deep
gossip

To the Princeton queer community, with warm good wishes, Henry Abelove

deep
gossip

henry abelove

University of Minnesota Press
Minneapolis · London

Permission information for previously published material is on pages 103–4. Every effort has been made to obtain permission to reproduce copyright material in this book. If any proper acknowledgment has not been made, we encourage copyright holders to notify us.

Published by the University of Minnesota Press
111 Third Avenue South, Suite 290
Minneapolis, MN 55401-2520
http://www.upress.umn.edu

Library of Congress Cataloging-in-Publication Data

Abelove, Henry.
      Deep gossip / Henry Abelove.
           p.   cm.
      Includes bibliographical references.
      ISBN 0-8166-3826-8 (HC/j : alk. paper)
      1. Homosexuality—United States—History. 2. Homosexuality and literature—United States—History. 3. Matthiessen, F. O. (Francis Otto), 1902–1950. 4. Sex customs—England—History—18th century. 5. American literature—History and criticism. 6. Homosexuality in literature. 7. Gay and lesbian studies. I. Title.
      HQ76.3.U5A24 2003
      306.76'6'0973—dc21

                                                                    2003007371

Printed in the United States of America on acid-free paper

The University of Minnesota is an equal-opportunity educator and employer.

12 11 10 09 08 07 06 05 04 03   10 9 8 7 6 5 4 3 2 1

to

Lisa Duggan

Contents

Acknowledgments

No man was ever more honored in the character of
his raisers than I. They are destined, I trust, to assist at
the raising of loftier structures one day.
—HENRY DAVID THOREAU

Generous colleagues and loving friends helped me to write *Deep Gossip*. They encouraged me, answered questions for me, taught me lessons of many sorts, and with wit, patience, and kindness alleviated the pains of writing. I am glad to have this opportunity to extend my thanks to Steven Angelides, Nancy Armstrong, John Beynon, Chris Brasel, Dianne Chisholm, Eric Clarke, William A. Cohen, Christina Crosby, Michael Davidson, Jason Dewees, Steven Evans, John Guillory, Phillip Brian Harper, Neil Hertz, Neville Hoad, Janet Jakobsen, Claudia Johnson, Walter Johnson, Shu Kuge, M. Grazia Lolla, Steven Maynard, Jennifer Moxley, Greg Mullins, Kevin Murphy, Deborah Nelson, Jeff Nunokawa, Tavia Nyong'o, Richard Ohmann, Claire Potter, Jordan Rau, Joseph W. Reed Jr., Robert Reynolds, Ellen Rooney, Phyllis Rose, Gayle Rubin, Joan Wallach Scott, Eve Kosofsky Sedgwick, Todd Shepard, Nikhil Pal Singh, James Steakley, Marc Stein, John Wood Sweet, Leonard Tennenhouse, Michael Trask, Stephen Trask, Carole Vance, John Vincent, Clarence E. Walker, Tim Walton, Dorothy Wang, Stephen D. White, and especially Lisa Duggan. She helped most of all.

I am obliged to Jesse Ashlock and Peter Karys, who did library chores; to David Boshko, Susan Ferris, Brenda Keating, and Jackie Rich, who did word processing; to Edward Mendelson (literary executor of the estate of W. H. Auden), the William Morris Literary Agency (literary executor of the estate of Robert Penn Warren), Maureen Granville-Smith (administratrix of the estate of Frank O'Hara), HarperCollins, Penguin Ltd., Warner Bros. Publications U.S., and Alfred E. Knopf (a division of Random House, Inc.), for permission to quote writings; to Dr. Richard Hyde, who pointed me to the papers of Russell Cheney and F. O. Matthiessen on deposit at the Beinecke Library, Yale University; and to the Vassar College Library, *Monthly Review,* Bettye-Lane, and Rick Stafford, who permitted the reproduction of photographs.

Introduction
Deep Gossip

When the poet Frank O'Hara was accidentally killed at Fire Island in 1966, Allen Ginsberg memorialized him with an elegy titled "City Midnight Junk Strains." In that elegy, Ginsberg described O'Hara as a "Curator of funny emotions" and drew attention to his "ear." It was "a common ear," he wrote, "for our deep gossip."

I want to begin this book by reflecting on the words Ginsberg used to describe O'Hara. My purpose isn't to provide a reading of Ginsberg's elegy. What I aim to do instead is to say why these long-ago words of description, composed by one queer man for another, seem to me, as a writer and teacher of lesbian, gay, queer topics, so resonant still.

CURATOR (FROM THE LATIN, *CURA,* "CARE, CONCERN"). O'Hara held a job as a curator at the Museum of Modern Art. But here the word "curator" has a reach that extends beyond the job to encompass a whole life's work. Yet writers and intellectuals like O'Hara are rarely represented primarily as caretakers. More usually, perhaps, they represent themselves, or others represent them, as creators, or as innovators, or as discoverers or expounders of truth, or as contributors to knowledge or understanding, or as contenders against falsehood or ignorance. I take it that the curator's life doesn't exclude these other roles. After all, a curator may need to create, innovate, discover, expound, contribute, or contend in order to take care effectively. What the word emphasizes, though, isn't the other, probably more familiar roles. It emphasizes conservation, nurturance, scrupulosity. For a caretaker, these would come first.

FUNNY EMOTIONS. Here the word "funny" has at least two distinct connotations. Emotions are funny when, on the one hand, they are associated with fun or pleasure, and when, on the other, they are likely to be made fun of—mocked, derided, trivialized, even stigmatized. Because they are likely to be made fun of, they require care. To take care of them is, however, to do something different from therapy, and the word "curator" points the difference sharply. Curating, taking care of, isn't curing—or wanting to cure—or supposing or imagining that a cure is needed.

A COMMON EAR. This, I take it, is a capacity and willingness to listen with close attention democratically, for instance, to all those high or low, extraordinary or ordinary, within one's own circle and kind, or outside of both, who experience and express funny emotions and with them make lives.

OUR DEEP GOSSIP. Here gossip is illicit speculation, information, knowledge. It is an indispensable resource for those who are in any sense or measure disempowered, as those who experience funny emotions may be, and it is deep whenever it circulates in subterranean ways and touches on matters hard to grasp and of crucial concern. But who are the "we" that make up the antecedent of "our"—the "we" to whom the deep gossip belongs? No "we" is defined or specified here. None is even mentioned. So the antecedent of "our" is left suggestively indefinite, unfixed, open.

In Ginsberg's terms of description for O'Hara—*Curator of funny emotions, a common ear for our deep gossip*—I believe I hear the intimation of an intellectual vocation. For me, this vocation is an aspiration rather than an achievement. No one knows better or more fully than I do how very far short of the achievement I fall. I take this occasion to muster the hopes that animate a life, maybe also a tradition, and the essays that follow.

The essays are arranged here in the order in which they were completed—the first of them in 1980, some twenty-three years ago, the last, just this year.

When I wrote the first, "Freud, Male Homosexuality, and the Americans," I knew, and wanted others to know, that many U.S. American psychoanalysts held firmly to the damaging view that men who had sex with men were psychologically disordered, sick, and in need of cure. I also knew that these many psychoanalysts liked to claim that Freud had authorized this view of theirs, that his clinical findings provided the warrant and justification for it, and that they and he were at one. But they were not at one with Freud. In my essay I undertook to show that there was little basis in Freud's writings, published or unpublished, for the view that sex between men was pathological. I also showed that Freud had been persistently and mordantly critical of the tendency of U.S. American psychoanalysts to see pathology wherever they encountered what they believed to be immorality.

To take from these psychoanalysts their claim of union with Freud was one of my purposes. But I had other purposes, too. I also wanted to clear the way back to Freud for those persons deterred from reading him by the psychoanalysts who had claimed wrongly to speak in his name. I was convinced then, and I am still convinced, that in Freud's work there are lessons that are valuable and nourishing even for those whom the U.S. American psychoanalysts tried to pathologize. One such lesson seemed to me to be especially pertinent, and I highlighted it in my essay. Freud argued, in direct opposition to the homosexual emancipation movement of his own day, that homosexuals constituted no "special variety" of humankind, no "distinct sexual species." I very much wanted to bring that genuinely Freudian lesson into discussion within the lesbian/gay civil rights movement, which was active in 1980 when the essay was composed and has been active since then as well.

In that first essay, I probed the history of a set of pseudo-Freudian and Freudian views on sex. In my next essay, "Some Speculations on the History of Sexual Intercourse during the Long Eighteenth Century in England," I turned to the history of sexual conduct. Focusing on the period 1680 to 1830 in England and on cross-sex sexual practices, I advanced a series of new hypotheses. I won't repeat those hypotheses here; instead, I will reflect on some of the circumstances in which the essay was produced.

It was written in 1988 and 1989, as the AIDS epidemic raged and as a strong political resistance to AIDS took shape. Among those resisting, one widely shared and hard-won conclusion was this: sexual practice is not historically invariant; it is not fixed. It does change; it can change. A particular sexual behavior may become less popular, another, more. I carried this conclusion with me as an insight into my study of the English past, and I applied the insight to cross-sex sexual practices, as these were revealed by a mass of demographic data. In analyzing the data, I found that what I termed "sexual intercourse so-called" (penis in vagina, vagina around penis, with seminal emission uninterrupted) had become increasingly popular in England during the long eighteenth century. That this change in sexual practice, this rising popularity of sexual intercourse so-called, is hard to see, is part of my argument. The immense weight of privilege that has long accrued to sexual intercourse so-called has made its vicissitudes virtually invisible. It is almost always imagined as a constant. I learned how to imagine it differently among AIDS resisters during the early years of the epidemic.

One of my aims, then, was to demonstrate the contingency of sexual intercourse so-called. Another was to find a way to think cogently about sex in the past without relying on the concept of identity. I did not want to write about gay identity, straight identity, or identity in any of its familiar uses. Like everyone else who studied sex in the past, I had benefited enormously from the outstanding books and articles that had taken as their topic the emergence and development of sexual identity, especially lesbian and gay identity. I admired these books and articles; I admire them still. But I did not accept that the concept of identity on which they depend was wholly satisfactory. It was interesting. It was suggestive. It was—in the hands of the authors of these books and articles—well deployed and illuminating. Yet "identity," as for instance in the term "gay identity," struck me as a misnomer. "Identity" connotes or suggests sameness, and the concept of identity seemed to me to posit more coherence, homogeneity, and unity than I thought was possible or even desirable. I heard the term as imperious, peremptory—much more so than, say, "subculture," or even "community." Grateful for what had been achieved in history writing with the aid of the concept of identity, I nevertheless felt myself called away from all that. I meant my essay to be as telling for what it omitted as for what it included.

While reflecting on the books and articles on sexual identity, I also assigned them in the courses I taught. How queer students responded to these reading assignments fascinated me. I decided to write about their response, and I titled the essay that resulted "The Queering of Lesbian/Gay History."

I had noticed that queer students, who were increasingly numerous in my university from the late 1980s on, tended to differ in outlook, at least in some ways, from the lesbian and gay students whom I had taught in preceding years. My aim was to describe carefully the outlook of the queer students, and since they tended to be strongly critical of the reading assigned to them on sexual identity, I was especially concerned with explaining their critique.

This critique seemed worthwhile, even important. Yet I belonged to the generation of historians who had produced the work on sexual identity; I had been influenced, maybe even partly formed, by that work; and I valued it, despite my reservations about it. So I shared something both with it and with the queer critique so vividly urged by my students. In my essay I hoped to mediate between that work and that critique—to find some common ground between them, preserving what was strong in each. Whether I realized that hope in any measure must, of course, be for others to say.

In 1991 I left my teaching job for a year and took up a research fellowship in Salt Lake City, Utah. While I was there I joined a small political organization, Queer Nation/Salt Lake City, and I wrote about it in my essay "From Thoreau to Queer Politics." My aim was to analyze the queer politics in which I was so eagerly participating—its lineage, its direction, and its significance. That the particular queer organization about which I wrote was based in a provincial city in the Mountain West seemed to me to be an advantage. Very little had been written previously concerning queer political work, and the little that was available focused on big cities like New York, Chicago, Toronto. I hoped to widen the lens through which queer life was viewed and represented.

In thinking about the politics of Queer Nation/Salt Lake City, I found myself recalling Thoreau's *Walden*. From my point of view, *Walden* and Queer Nation/Salt Lake City belonged together, in a singular and distinguished tradition of political theory and action. To say why I thought so, I had to expound *Walden* and Thoreau as well, displacing the Emersonian reading of both of them—the reading that had predominated in both academic and popular circles since Thoreau's death. I also had to give serious and scrupulous attention to the *meaningfulness* of queer politics. It was perhaps unusual to look for meaning there. I knew that in the conventional view political groups like Queer Nation were silly, diversionary, pointless. Their only use might be as therapy for their members. That this conventional and condescending view is blind is a leading implication of my essay.

My study of Thoreau led me to think further about mid-nineteenth-century American writings on democracy and about their expositors and critics as well. It seemed to me that some of the most significant questions that these writings raise had been persistently deflected in an influential strain of American Studies scholarship. In my next essay, "American Studies, Queer Studies," I tried to show how and why these questions had been deflected, and with what results. My strategy was to take a close look at the life and career of F. O. Matthiessen, one of the founders of American Studies as a discipline; at his great book on American democratic culture in the mid–nineteenth century, *American Renaissance*; and at the writings that had responded to it, explicitly or implicitly, since its first publication in 1941.

Matthiessen had long been an object of interest for me. When I arrived as a freshman at Harvard College in 1962, he had been dead only twelve years. His name and reputation were still a present force there. I read *American Renaissance* with excitement during my first semester, heard stories told about him, too, some hostile, some adulatory, and I remember that I wondered: Was he really gay, as rumor had it? Did he really kill himself, and if so, why? What were his politics? Why had he been so much reviled, so much treasured?

Returning to Matthiessen thirty-six years later, poring over his unpublished letters and papers in the Beinecke Library at Yale, studying once again his published writings, considering the many and varied important responses to his work, trying to satisfy the curiosity about him I had first felt when I was young: all this brought me pleasure. But it also gave me, I believe, a useful perspective on what the discipline of American Studies is, has been, and might yet be.

In my most recent essay, "New York City Gay Liberation and the Queer Commuters," I turned to the topic of gay liberation. Perhaps I should rather say that I returned to it, because from the time I began to write these essays it has never been far from my thoughts. Gay liberation, I should explain, was a social and political movement of the late 1960s and early 1970s. Its impact, not only in the United States but also throughout the world, has been powerful and ramifying, yet it is rarely recognized or acknowledged. Its outlook and its values are also largely unknown. When it is mentioned, it is perhaps most typically represented as a series of small-scale militant protests, starting with the Stonewall riot of 1969. Or sometimes it is represented as just a precursor of the later and perhaps more commonly respected lesbian/gay civil rights movement. But gay liberation was far more than militant protest, far more, too, than the precursor of a civil rights movement.

In my essay, I hoped to recover and preserve something of gay liberation's actual flavor and point. I also hoped to explore the relations between liberationism and literature. I tried to show that the rhetoric of gay liberation had been drawn from the queer-inflected anglophone literature of the 1950s and 1960s. Without it, gay liberation could never have been. I gave particular attention to James Baldwin, Elizabeth Bishop, Paul Bowles, Jane Bowles, William Burroughs, Allen Ginsberg, Paul Goodman, Frank O'Hara, and Ned Rorem. During the post–World War II era, nearly all of these authors left or were driven out of the United States for long periods of time. While they were abroad, they observed the forces of decolonization, so importantly active in so many sites then. In their novels and stories and poems and memoirs and journals, these authors all represented same-sex eroticism. Most represented the struggles of decolonization, too. In reading the various writings of these authors, the liberationists of the 1960s and 1970s learned how to say what they wanted to say politically about same-sex eroticism and the global history of their times as well.

A conviction that *funny emotions* should be genuinely valued, and *deep gossip* genuinely shared, is a motive of each of the essays collected here. That *funny emotions* lead the way to *deep gossip*, and that *deep gossip* fosters *funny emotions*, is the theme of the book.

Of the essays that follow, four have been previously published. All six deal with the history of sexuality—especially gay, lesbian, queer sexuality—in relation to culture and to politics.

Finally, a note on terminology: Throughout these essays, I use many different terms of description for bodies and sexualities. I refer to lesbians, queers, perverts, homosexuals, inverts, butches, femmes, gay men, and more. In deciding which term to use when several might seem to be applicable—for instance, "gay" and "homosexual"—I try to follow the preference or custom in terminology of the people whose past lives and works I am then discussing.

Freud, Male Homosexuality, and the Americans

Anybody inquiring about Freud's attitude to homosexuality will soon come across a letter he wrote in April 1935. The letter is now almost famous. It was first printed in 1951, it has been reprinted since many times, and it is conveniently available in Ernest Jones's standard biography. Freud wrote it in English as a courtesy to his correspondent who was an American, a mother, distressed and embarrassed because her young son was homosexual. What the letter tells her is that she has less cause for distress than she may think and none whatsoever for embarrassment:

> I gather [Freud says] ... that your son is a homosexual. I am most impressed by the fact that you do not mention this term yourself in your information about him. May I question you, why you avoid it? Homosexuality is assuredly no advantage, but it is nothing to be ashamed of, no vice, no degradation, it cannot be classified as an illness, we consider it to be a variation of the sexual function produced by a certain arrest of sexual development.

He goes on to say more:

1

Many highly respectable individuals of ancient and modern times have been homosexuals, several of the greatest men among them. (Plato, Michelangelo, Leonardo da Vinci, etc.) It is a great injustice to persecute homosexuality as a crime and a cruelty too. If you do not believe me, read the books of Havelock Ellis.

By asking me if I can help, you mean, I suppose, if I can abolish homosexuality and make normal heterosexuality take its place. The answer is, in a general way, we cannot promise to achieve it. In a certain number of cases we succeed in developing the blighted germs of heterosexual tendencies which are present in every homosexual, in the majority of cases it is no more possible. It is a question of the quality and the age of the individual. The result of treatment cannot be predicted.

What analysis can do for your son runs in a different line. If he is unhappy, neurotic, torn by conflicts, inhibited in his social life, analysis may bring him harmony, peace of mind, full efficiency, whether he remains a homosexual or gets changed. If you make up your mind he should have analysis with me—I don't expect you will—he has to come over to Vienna. I have no intention of leaving here. However, don't neglect to give me your answer.

Sincerely yours with kind wishes

Freud[1]

The American mother said that she was grateful for the letter, sent a copy eventually to the sex researcher Alfred Kinsey, and told him that Freud was a "great and good" man. Presumably she found the letter helpful, maybe also comforting, even though it had probed her fearfulness and prejudice. Jones is probably right to describe the letter, in his biography, as a remarkable "kindness."[2] After all, Freud had no previous acquaintance with the woman, yet he took the time to write to her when he was himself deathly ill.

But the letter was more than just a "kindness." It was also the considered expression of a viewpoint that Freud had long deeply felt and tenaciously held. Everything about homosexuality that he says in the letter had been an article of conviction with him for more than thirty years. Summarized: homosexuality is no advantage; it is also no illness; it should be neither prosecuted as a crime nor regarded as a disgrace; no homosexual need be treated psychoanalytically unless he also, and quite incidentally, happened to be neurotic. Freud had often expressed himself on the subject before, and on occasion very publicly.

As early as 1903 he had given an interview to the Vienna newspaper *Die Zeit*, which was doing a feature story on a local scandal: a prominent Vienna professional man was on trial, charged with homosexual practices. A reporter had come to get Freud's reaction, and Freud had said:

> I advocate the standpoint that the homosexual does not belong before the tribunal of a court of law. I am even of the firm conviction that homosexuals must not be treated as sick people, for a perverse orientation is far from being a sickness. Wouldn't that oblige us to characterize as *sick* many great thinkers and scholars whom we admire precisely because of their mental health?

He had then repeated himself, apparently for the sake of emphasis: *"Homosexual persons are not sick, but they also do not belong in a court of law!"* He had added finally, and by way of qualification, that if a homosexual molested a child below "the age of consent," then he should of course be charged in the courts, just as a heterosexual should be charged under analogous circumstances.[3]

In 1930 Freud again spoke in the Vienna public press on the subject of homosexuality. This time he appeared as a cosignatory to a statement addressed to a joint Austro-German legal commission, which was considering the revision of the penal code. Among the other signatories were Arthur Schnitzler, Franz Werfel, and Moritz Schlick. The statement noted that the commission was reported as deadlocked over a proposal to repeal the laws penalizing homosexual relations between "consenting adult males." But the deadlock should be broken. "Humanity, justice, and reason" all required the repeal, and it should be agreed to immediately. "Homosexuality," the statement continued, had "been present throughout history and among all peoples." The laws that penalized it represented an "extreme violation of human rights" for they denied homosexuals "their very sexuality." They also gave a wide opening to "blackmail" and indirectly drove some homosexuals to "suicide." There was yet another bad consequence of these laws. By stigmatizing homosexuality as "criminal," they often forced homosexuals into "antisocial" postures and attitudes. The statement concluded with the "demand" that homosexuals be allowed the same "rights" as everyone else.[4]

These were Freud's public interventions; privately he took a similar line. For instance, he held that there was no good reason why homosexuals should necessarily be refused permission to become psychoanalysts. Freud's position turned out to be objectionable to most of his associates. The issue surfaced in 1920 when the Dutch Psychoanalytic Association had an application for membership from a doctor known to be "manifestly homosexual." Uncertain how to respond, they turned for advice to a member of Freud's inner circle, Ernst Jones, the same who later wrote the standard biography. Jones kept Freud informed by letter. "I advised against it," he said, "and now I hear ... that the man has been detected and committed to prison." He then asked whether or not Freud thought that always to refuse homosexual applicants would be "a safe general maxim to act on." Freud consulted with another member of the inner circle, Otto Rank, who was also a close friend, and then Rank and Freud jointly wrote back to Jones and censured his propriety:

> Your query, dear Ernst, concerning prospective membership of homosexuals has been considered by us and we disagree with you. In effect we cannot exclude such persons without other sufficient reasons, as we cannot agree with their legal prosecution. We feel that a decision in such cases should depend upon a thorough examination of the other qualities of the candidate.

Rank and Freud wrote, of course, from Vienna. Jones, who got their letter, was in London. Within about a month, news of the exchange had reached the analysts of Berlin, whereupon three of them, Hanns Sachs, Karl Abraham, and Max Eitingon, all alarmed, wrote to Freud in criticism of his position.

The criticism was put tactfully but firmly: "We have not yet decided," they began, "about the question of admitting homosexual analysts to our Society." This was no doubt meant to remind Freud that the decision, at least in Berlin, was constitutionally theirs rather than his. "But," they went on, "we have had some thoughts on this matter." Their "thoughts" were that "homosexuality appears in many forms as part of a neurosis," that in such instances the homosexuality "should be analyzed," that neurotic homosexuals might and often did refuse to let their analysis go deep, and that when they so refused they could hardly turn out to be good analysts themselves. Sachs, Abraham, and Eitingon then concluded, "We agree that we only should accept homosexuals into our membership when they have other qualities in their favor." This conclusion both restated Freud's position and modified it subtly. His letter had stipulated that homosexuality ought to be a neutral factor or a nonfactor in the evaluation of applicants; their letter, on the other hand, suggested that homosexuality might well make for a presumption against an applicant but that he should nevertheless be admitted if he were judged good enough. The wording of both letters is, however, close, and Freud chose to be, or had to be, content with their response.[5]

As a clinician, Freud refused to treat homosexuals unless he thought them markedly neurotic.[6] Otherwise there was nothing to treat. Homosexuality was not in his view an illness, and whenever associates who assumed that it was an illness tried to refer homosexuals to him for treatment, he turned them away if he knew in advance that they were merely homosexuals. He could not always know in advance, and he must on occasion have had to see, if only for a single session, a patient who was homosexual and relatively unneurotic but forced to consult him by a psychiatrist, a family doctor, a friend, or a relative, like the American mother with whom Freud corresponded in 1935.

It would be interesting to know how he handled such patients; but he has left us no account of his dealings with any of them. For him they were not cases, and so there was no reason to write up a case history. But there is one account of a single session with Freud, written by a patient who may fit into this category. It is hard to be entirely sure; the account is moving as a portrait of the psychoanalyst but disappointingly sparse about the patient himself, whose name was Bruno Goetz. At the time Goetz consulted Freud, he was a student at the University of Vienna, an aspiring poet, poor, afflicted with eye trouble and bad headaches, and apparently sexually unconventional, too. One of his professors, who was worried about Goetz, had arranged for the consultation and sent Freud some of the man's poems as well. Goetz did not want to go, but the professor's authority was sufficient to make him, and he went.

Once Goetz got to Freud's office, he began to feel better immediately. The headaches disappeared, and he talked eagerly about his life and loves. He talked about masturbating, about once loving a woman older than himself, about his fascination with the sea, about his attraction to sailors, whom he wanted "to kiss," and about his not marrying. Freud said (as Goetz reports), "'And the matter with the sailors has never upset you?'" Goetz answered, "'Never . . . I was very much in love. And when you're in love, everything is fine. Right?'" Freud replied, "'For you certainly . . .' and laughed." Toward the end of the consultation, Freud asked Goetz when he had last eaten a steak. Goetz said four weeks before. Freud then handed him a sealed envelope, told him it was a "'prescription,'" and then turned "shy" as he concluded the session by saying: "'Please accept this envelope and allow me to play your father this time. A small fee for the joy you have brought me with your poems and the story of your youth.'" When Goetz left and opened the envelope, he found that it contained money, 200 kronen, more than enough to buy a big steak dinner.[7]

Freud was perfectly consistent on the subject of homosexuality. What he told the American mother in his letter of 1935, that it was neither advantage, crime, illness, nor disgrace, he had long believed and long acted on. His viewpoint was not wholeheartedly shared by most of his fellow analysts, though no analyst so far as I know directly and avowedly rejected it during Freud's lifetime. But his colleagues did show some hesitation about it, some edginess. The Dutch wondered whether or not a homosexual should be admitted to practice analysis; Jones, in England, thought not; the Berliners said maybe yes, maybe no, but were probably inclined to say no; and some analysts referred relatively unneurotic homosexuals to Freud for treatment, though he of course thought there was no need. Jung too may have felt rather differently from Freud on the subject of homosexuality. His viewpoint, during the years when he was still associated with psychoanalysis, is hard to reconstruct fully, but there is a suggestive comment in one of his letters.

Jung and Freud were corresponding about where a certain essay of Freud's was to be published. The *Zeitschrift für Sexualwissenschaft*, a journal edited by a homosexual, had been mentioned, and Jung advised against using it. "If the '175ers' are in charge, that will hardly be a guarantee of its scientific attitude," Jung wrote. In the German law code the number of the clause in which the penalties for homosexual practice were specified was 175.[8] The term "175ers" meant homosexuals and was derogatory. Jung's comment, in substance, was also prejudicious. Freud replied by saying that he had not intended the essay for the *Zeitschrift*, which might become the voice of the homosexual emancipation movement in Germany, and therefore might be too political. He said that he had intended the essay for the *Jahrbuch für Sexuelle Zwischenstufen*, another journal edited by the same homosexual who edited the *Zeitschrift*. Jung made no further comment.[9]

So far as I can tell, only three analysts can be tentatively identified as sharing without reservation in Freud's attitude toward homosexuality. They are Rank, who cosigned the letter to Jones calling for the admission of qualified homosexuals to the practice of psychoanalysis; Isidor Sadger, whose position can be deduced from some essays he published;[10] and Victor Tausk. One of Tausk's colleagues reported him as saying this in about 1914 on the treatment of a particular neurotic homosexual: "his therapeutic goal for the patient was to rid him of feelings of guilt about his homosexuality so that he could be free to satisfy his homosexual needs."[11] But if Rank, Sadger, and Tausk stood firmly with Freud in this matter, they were the exceptions. Most analysts had room for other thoughts.

It was in America, however, that Freud's viewpoint on homosexuality was least accepted or maybe most resisted. Jung may in a careless moment have let slip a prejudicious slur; Jones may have wanted to draw the line at having homosexual colleagues; the Dutch and Germans may also have felt some of his reserve; but from the very beginnings of the transplanting of psychoanalysis onto these shores, American analysts have tended to view homosexuality with disapproval and have actually wanted to get rid of it altogether. As early as 1916, when Freud was still very active, Smith Ely Jeliffe, a prominent New York analyst and a founder of the *Psychoanalytic Review*, declared that "individual training" and "education" should control the "homogenic" tendency and "direct it" to a "normal, well-adjusted sexual life" so that there need be no homosexuality.[12]

Jeliffe's declaration is perhaps distinctively American; it reflects the outlook that historians usually call moralistic and that has always dominated psychoanalytic thinking in this country. It is an outlook that Freud knew, despised, and opposed, but never succeeded in overcoming or even mitigating. Why he never succeeded may require an explanation. He was, after all, a domineering leader, with little patience for any deviationism, and presumably he could have cut off the offending American analysts, just as he eventually cut off such Europeans as Adler and Jung. Perhaps he was afraid that too much severity on the American front would put the whole future of psychoanalysis at risk. It was clear, certainly by the 1930s, that the movement was going to grow fastest in America. He may also have held back partly out of a kind of indifference. What Americans said and thought was less important to him than what his fellow Europeans said and thought. Then, too, he believed that the American analysts' outlook was not accidental but necessary, derived directly from what he took to be the root conditions of American life. If that were true, what good could come of cutting off particular analysts?

Still, he argued with them, teased, parried. His most frequent butt was James Jackson Putnam of Harvard, the American analyst whom he liked most or maybe disliked least. Their correspondence, stretching over a period of about seven years, was on Freud's part one long effort to get Putnam to relinquish his moralism (specific allusions to homosexuality, or indeed any sexuality, hardly came up, so elevated were Putnam's ideas, so obliging was Freud as a correspondent); on Putnam's part it was one long refusal.

Putnam met Freud in 1909 and had on that occasion apparently been firmly told that he should not try to hold up before his analytic patients some ethical goal of his own. "It still appears to me," he wrote later that year, "that . . . the psychoanalytic method needs to be supplemented by methods which seek to hold up before the patient some goal toward which he may strive." Putnam went on to note that he was currently treating a "lady" who was "a great sufferer from morbid self-consciousness and blushing," that he was making "good headway" in tracing out the origins of her "symptoms," but that he had found himself confronted by the "difficulty" that she had "lost all interest in life and living." Should he not try, in a hortatory way, to provide her with such an interest? Freud replied that no analyst could "compensate" a patient for giving up an "illness." But that was not the analyst's fault.

What would you have us do when a woman complains about her thwarted life, when, with youth gone, she notices that she has been deprived of the joy of loving for merely conventional reasons? She is quite right, and we stand helpless before her, for we cannot make her young again. But the recognition of our therapeutic limitations reinforces our determination to change other social factors so that men and women shall no longer be forced into hopeless situations.

This was Freud at his most militantly political; American moralism always brought it out in him. But the militancy made no apparent impact on Putnam, who soon wrote back that patients need "more than to simply learn to know themselves," they need also to know the "reasons why they should adopt higher views of their obligations." He wrote back yet again: "As I study patients and try to relieve them of their symptoms, I find that I must also try to improve their moral characters and temperaments." Soon after, he told Freud one of his childhood fantasies—it was of a happy family life—and asked for an interpretation. This request gave Freud an opening that he gleefully took:

> On the whole I see that you are suffering from a too early and too strongly repressed sadism expressed in over-goodness and self-torture. Behind the fantasy of a happy family life, you would discover the normal repressed fantasies of rich sexual fulfillment.

Later Freud responded again on a note less personal but still very naughty, gibing at the Christian rhetoric that lay just below the surface of Putnam's letters:

> You make psychoanalysis seem so much nobler and more beautiful: in her Sunday clothes I scarcely recognize the servant who performs my household tasks.

Next, undaunted, Putnam wrote to say that he wanted to compose something rather big on the subject of "sublimation," with special reference "to the work of Dante and Emerson." Freud replied that he looked forward to it "with great interest." Putnam then wrote more about his personal commitment to sublimation and to the task of helping his patients achieve it satisfactorily. Freud replied this time with bitterness rather than irony: "As soon," he wrote, as analysts take on "the task of leading the patient toward sublimation, they hasten away from the arduous tasks of psychoanalysis so that they can take up the much more comfortable . . . duties of the teacher and paragon of virtue." Finally Freud turned very direct. He dropped all obliquity, all his tones except candor, and in one of the last few letters he wrote to Putnam, shortly before Putnam's death separated them forever, attacked his moralism straight on:

> Sexual morality as society—and at its most extreme, American society—defines it, seems very despicable to me. I stand for a much freer sexual life.

That, too, made no apparent impact on Putnam, and in his next letter he ignored altogether Freud's remark about America.[13]

If Freud thought that American sexual morality was despicable, he also thought he knew how it had come to be that way. He visited America only once, in the fall of 1909, to deliver five introductory lectures on psychoanalysis at Clark University to an audience that, incidentally, included both William James and Emma Goldman. During his stay he got to see New York, New Haven, Boston, Worcester, and Niagara Falls, and he also spent some time in the Adirondacks. Still, the trip was brief, the itinerary limited, and his conclusions were exceptionally positive and firm. No doubt he had made up his mind at least tentatively before the trip had begun, largely on the basis of his reading and his personal contacts with individual Americans, partly probably on the basis of the prejudice against America that is always common in European intellectual circles.

When asked after he returned to Vienna what exactly he thought was wrong here, he would usually treat the question as unserious and respond lightly. He hated the food; it gave him indigestion. Or he might say he hated the accent; only the British knew how to speak English right. But sometimes he treated the question as serious and responded accordingly, and there is no difficulty in making out his actual view. First of all, he thought that Americans were extraordinarily overrepressed. He found them sexually vapid, flavorless. As his Viennese colleague Paul Federn tactlessly reported years later in 1947 when he spoke in New York at the dedication of a Freud bust in the headquarters of the New York Psychoanalytic Society, Freud had always held that in America there was not "enough libido actually to be found and felt by him."[14] Why were the Americans such nonentities sexually? Because they sublimated their sexual energy so completely. As for their despicable moralism, that was the rationale for the sublimation. And was the goal of American sublimation the production of art, science, law, architecture, music, literature? No: the goal was cash, acquisition, accumulation. All the energy that was not loosed sexually was going toward making money and toward very little else. Jones, in his biography, put the point delicately: Freud had an "unfavorable impression" of America. "I imagine," Jones said, "that the aversion had something to do with a feeling that commercial success dominated the scale of values in the United States."[15]

Freud himself put the point still more delicately, but nonetheless very definitely, while actually speaking to his American audience at Clark. To be sure, his primary rhetorical strategy in those five lectures was to flatter his hearers in the hopes of securing their favorable interest in what he had to say concerning psychoanalysis. He told them that theirs was a "New World"; he added that in the old, benighted European world there was unreasoning prejudice against psychoanalysis; and he intimated that in the New World no such prejudice was likely. He told them that he had originally planned to speak chiefly about "dream interpretation" but after consideration had rejected the plan. It seemed to him, he said, somehow wrong to focus on dreams in a country so admirably "devoted to practical aims." He told them that "hysteria" might perhaps be best understood as analogous to a kind of overinvolvement in history.

Imagine, Freud said, a "Londoner" unable to live joyfully in the present because he could not escape from the clutch of the past and so spent all his time mourning at spots like "Charing Cross" or "the Monument," consecrated to ancient losses. In developing this analogy, Freud was hinting broadly and quite mendaciously that since Americans had much less history than, say, Londoners, they were much better off. All this was flattery, and thickly applied, too. But in the midst of the flattery, Freud also managed to say what he thought. His moment came when he explained how jokes were to be interpreted psychoanalytically. First he gave an example of a joke:

> Two not particularly scrupulous businessmen had succeeded, by dint of a series of highly risky enterprises, in amassing a large fortune, and they were now making efforts to push their way into good society. One method, which struck them as a likely one, was to have their portraits painted by the most celebrated and highly paid artist in the city. . . . The precious canvasses were shown for the first time at a large evening party, and the two hosts led the most influential connoisseur . . . up to the wall on which the portraits were hanging side by side. He studied the works for a long time, and then, shaking his head, as though there was something he had missed, pointed to the gap between the pictures and asked quietly: "But where's the Savior?"

The audience laughed. Freud went on:

> Clearly what the connoisseur meant to say was: "You are a couple of rogues, like the two thieves between whom the Savior was crucified." But he did not say this. Instead he made a remark which seems at first `sight strangely inappropriate . . . , but which we recognize later . . . as an *allusion* to the insult that he had in mind.

Having explained how to interpret the joke, Freud proceeded to ask: "Why" did the connoisseur "not tell the rogues straight out what he wanted to say?" Why did he tell them only indirectly via the joke? He then answered his own question. The connoisseur had "excellent counter-motives working against his desire to say it to their faces. There are risks attendant upon insulting people who are one's hosts."[16]

It takes but a moment's reflection to realize that at Clark, Freud was the honored guest, the Americans were his hosts, and he was insulting them, though indirectly, with the joke he told. They were the unscrupulous businessmen; they were the thieves. From this opinion of them, or rather of us, as thieves—and consequently also as sexless and despicably moralistic—Freud never budged.

What happened to homosexuals who found themselves in treatment with American psychoanalysts of the era of Putnam and Jeliffe—Putnam, who thought he should inspire his patients with his own ethical vision; Jeliffe, who thought that training and education should control homosexual feeling and reshape it into "normal, well-adjusted" sexuality? First of all, such patients could feel physically safe; they ran no risk, as long as they were in the hands of the analysts, of getting castrated. This disaster sometimes overtook homosexuals in nonanalytic treatment. Analysts only talked. Just what the talk was we cannot now know exactly and fully. But we can know partially, fragmentarily, a small sample of it, a sample that concerns an American homosexual named C. M. Otis, who in 1911 found himself in successive consultations with two different Boston analysts, Isador Coriat and Louville Emerson.

Emerson took notes that are still extant. From them we learn that Otis described himself as having never had intercourse with a woman, as having more than occasionally had sexual contact with boys, as having long felt both persecuted and sure that he could never become heterosexual. Emerson saw Otis for six therapy sessions. During the sixth Emerson ended their connection. In his notes he recorded the reason for his making so decisive and abrupt an ending: the patient "shows no adequate emotional reaction to my suggestions." He did not specify what the suggestions were.[17] Some eight years later Emerson published in the *Psychoanalytic Review* a brief and courteous critique of Freud. The point of the critique was that Freud was wrong to try to exclude "ethics" from psychoanalysis. All analysts must try to tell which social relations were, and which were not, "righteous."[18] Whatever were the suggestions that Emerson made and Otis rejected, we can surely conclude that Otis's experience with his analyst was significantly different from Goetz's with his.

To return to Freud's letter to the American mother. His motive in writing it was by no means just "kindness," nor was it just a determination to restate a position he had long held. He wanted also to hit back at us Americans, at our moralism and our misuse of psychoanalysis. He knew perfectly well that the letter would be noticed. He intended it to be noticed. It was a deliberate provocation, and perhaps the heart of it was the passage where he ended: "If you make up your mind he should have analysis with me—I don't expect you will—he has to come over to Vienna."[19] Freud had no need of more patients, and the woman was a stranger. His object was to tell her, and everybody else, too, that her son could not be properly treated in America.

It may be surprising, in the light of what this essay has said so far, to find that Freud was very much at odds with the homosexual emancipation movement of his own day. But he was. On one important matter he disagreed adamantly with the line taken by the movement, and he expressed the disagreement in his psychological writings on three separate occasions.

The movement was then based mostly in Germany, where it originated during the latter part of the nineteenth century. Its progenitor was Karl Heinrich Ulrichs (1825–1895), a Hanoverian lawyer who in a series of books propounded the view that homosexuals constituted "a third sex," possessed of a "female soul" in a "male body." Ulrichs's spiritual successor and the movement's first great leader was Magnus Hirschfeld (1868–1935), a Jewish doctor in Berlin, who as publicist, organizer, lobbyist, and clinical investigator worked long and tirelessly for the repeal of the laws penalizing homosexuality and for public recognition of its widespread incidence. Like Ulrichs, Hirschfeld also thought of homosexuals as a biologically and psychically distinct group. He called them "sexual intermediates."[20]

As we have seen, Freud willingly endorsed the movement's law reform objectives. What he rejected was the theory that lay behind them, the theory of the "third sex," of "sexual intermediates." In

Three Essays on the Theory of Sexuality (1905), he criticized Ulrichs directly, referring to him by name as "a spokesman of the male inverts," and mentioned his notion of "a feminine brain in a masculine body" in order to brush it aside.[21] In *Leonardo da Vinci* (1910), he again took note of the movement's line:

> Homosexual men, who have in our times taken vigorous action against the restrictions imposed by law on their sexual activity, are fond of representing themselves, through their theoretical spokesmen, as being from the outset a distinct sexual species, as an intermediate sexual stage, as a "third sex."

He added that this representation should be viewed with "some reserve" for it took no account of the findings of psychoanalysis. Later, in the 1919 edition, he inserted in a footnote a firmer critical comment: "those who speak for homosexuals in the field of science have been incapable of learning anything from the established findings of psychoanalysis."[22] Yet again in *Introductory Lectures* (1917), he made much the same point. He said that homosexuals "through the mouth of their scientific spokesmen" were endeavoring to "represent themselves as a special variety of the human species—a 'third sex.'" This representation was, however, mistaken; psychoanalysis proved it wrong.[23]

But how did psychoanalysis prove it wrong? Freud thought that analysis showed that all people were "capable of making a homosexual object choice" and that all had "in fact made one in their unconscious." He thought that analysis also showed that

> libidinal attachments to persons of the same sex play no less a part in normal mental life, and a greater part as a motive force for illness, than do similar attachments to the opposite sex.[24]

With these findings in mind, he could hardly accept that homosexuals were "a distinct sexual species" or "a special variety of the human species." On the contrary, Freud held that all people were psychologically like the ones called homosexuals. No doubt homosexual men would on the whole tend to have sex with men, while nonhomosexual men would on the whole tend to have sex with women. This difference, though of "practical significance," was of small "theoretical" significance.[25] What was theoretically significant, what must never be forgotten or denied or elided, was that everybody's sexuality was homosexual in large part. Homosexuals, Freud insisted, were not "exceptions," and psychoanalysis was "decidedly opposed to any attempt" to separate them off "from the rest of mankind as a group of a special character."[26] To do so would be to reject, in fact to repress, the psychoanalytic theory of sex.

So Freud argued, but the movement was not much interested in his argument. Notions like the "third sex" or, to glance ahead for a moment to modern-day America, "gay people" can play an important role in enabling homosexual assertiveness. It is bracing to think of oneself as part of a group. One feels less odd, maybe less vulnerable, maybe even prouder. Besides, groups can organize to advance their members' common interests. In a parliamentary culture, as the Germany of Freud's day in some measure was, or as modern-day America is, group-organizational strength can often translate directly into political influence. Freud understood all this, and he cannot have been surprised when the homosexual emancipation movement ignored him. But he took his stand against their line anyway, just as he had also taken his stand against American moralism, and for the same reason: both line and moralism were, as he saw the matter, in effect repressions.

Freud died in 1939, four years after he had written his letter to the American mother. Almost as soon as he was cremated, a host of revisionist essays started rolling off the psychoanalytic presses, especially in America. One of the subjects most eagerly canvassed was homosexuality. I here review briefly and in a very foreshortened way what the American analysts said about it once they could be sure that Freud was gone.

Sandor Rado (1890–1972), of the Columbia Psychoanalytic Clinic in New York, was the first to declare himself. In a series of pieces published in the 1940s, he argued that male-female pairing was healthy, that it was moreover the "standard pattern," that homosexuality was an illness based on a fear of women, and that it could often be cured in psychoanalysis.[27]

Following Rado's lead, Irving Bieber (b. 1908) conducted a big study in the 1950s and published his results in 1962. His purpose was not, he said, to establish that homosexuality was an illness. All "psychoanalytic theories," he went on, effectually ignoring Freud, "*assume* that homosexuality is psychopathologic." His purpose was rather to come to understand the etiology of the illness; and he argued that it derived primarily from a certain sort of bad family situation: a domineering mother, a cold father. He too was relatively optimistic about achieving cures.

Charles Socarides (b. 1922) went furthest perhaps of any of the American analysts. He argued, in a series of pieces published mostly in the 1960s, that homosexuality was in fact a severe illness, accompanied often by such psychotic manifestations as schizophrenia or manic-depressive mood swings. While heterosexual pairings could make for "cooperation, solace, stimulation, enrichment, healthy challenge and fulfillment," homosexual pairings could bring only "destruction, mutual defeat, exploitation of the partner and the self, oral sadistic incorporation, aggressive onslaughts, attempts to alleviate anxiety, and a pseudo-solution to the aggressive and libidinal urges which dominate and torment the individual." Socarides also said that cures were possible.[28]

Influenced perhaps especially by Rado, the American Psychiatric Association (APA) in 1952 formally classified homosexuality as an illness. When the gay liberation movement grew strong in America in the 1960s, this classification, still very much on the books,[29] became a major issue for its members, and they devoted much effort to getting it rescinded. Through a mix of agitation and argument, they eventually succeeded. In 1973 the APA removed homosexuality from its official list of illnesses.[30] In announcing the declassification, the president of the APA said that he hoped the result would be a "more accommodative climate of opinion for the homosexual minority in our country."[31] Here the word to note is "minority." What the president assumed was that homosexuals were indeed a minority, a group with a special character. He assumed as much both because the gay liberation movement was predictably saying so and because their psychoanalytic allies were loudly agreeing.

Psychoanalytic allies? Yes: the movement had such allies, of whom the two most influential were Judd Marmor (b. 1910) and Robert Stoller (b. 1924). During the 1960s and 1970s, both these analysts clashed repeatedly with the Bieber-Socarides set. Both, denying that homosexuality was an illness, described it instead as the sexual orientation of a minority. In so describing it, they of course rejected the view that Freud had thought theoretically crucial— the view that *everybody's* sexuality was in large part homosexual. Marmor put his rejection tactfully: Freud had held that homosexuality was a "universal trend." That view was not "illogical," but it was "non-operational" and should be discarded.[32] Stoller said much the same: by sticking to Freud's view we could never have clear grounds for saying of anybody that he was not homosexual. That would be troublesome. We would probably be well advised to revert to a "less complicated definition of homosexuality" and think of it as just the preserve of homosexuals, as "that state in which sexual practices are performed by preference, in conscious fantasy or in reality, with a person of the same sex."[33] So Marmor and Stoller both saw homosexuality as belonging to homosexuals alone, who were therefore different from everybody else, and thus a minority. But homosexuals were not necessarily ill any more than was any other minority—blacks, Hispanics, Jews—and they were entitled to be free of the stigma that official psychiatry had placed on them so unfairly. Of course, the corollary of the humane ascription of minority status was this: people outside the minority need no longer think of themselves as in some important way homosexual, too.

At the APA meetings that had led up to the eventual decision to rescind the classification of homosexuality as an illness, all of the major protagonists had been analysts. On the one side, Bieber and Socarides; on the other, Marmor and Stoller. A strange spectacle: two sets of moralistic analysts, each opposing the other, each claiming to stand in the tradition of Freud, and each espousing a position that Freud had himself rejected as wrong and repressive. In America, Freudianism continues as it began.

Some Speculations on the History of Sexual Intercourse during the Long Eighteenth Century in England

It has been known for many years that the population of England increased mightily during the period now called the "long eighteenth century"—the period stretching from the 1680s to the 1830s. In 1681 the population stood at about 4.93 million; in 1831, it was 13.28 million. But what hasn't been known with any certainty, at least until recently, was whether this extraordinary increase of people was due to a decline in mortality, to an increase in fertility, or to a combination of both. Historians, of course, have argued about the matter, some favoring one answer, some favoring another; but since their arguments have been based on scanty or broken data, nothing of what they have said could be really established and command general assent.

This arguing was stilled in 1981, when the demographers Wrigley and Schofield, both associated with the Cambridge Group for the History of Population and Social Structure, published their seven-hundred-some-page magnum opus on English population history. Their book virtually settled the question.[1] At last sufficient data had been gathered (the data came from more than four hundred parish registers), and a statistical technique sufficiently sophisticated for the job of interpreting them had been utilized (the technique is called "back-projection"). Two years later, in 1983, Wrigley repeated the findings of the book in short form in an article for the journal *Past and Present*. He called the article "The Growth of Population in Eighteenth-Century England: A Conundrum Resolved," and to the decisive-sounding title he may actually have been entitled.[2]

What the work of Wrigley and Schofield shows is that the mighty increase in English population during the long eighteenth century was due to a combination of a decline in mortality and a rise in fertility, but that of these two factors, the rise in fertility was much more important. It isn't that the decline in mortality was negligible. In the 1680s the average life expectancy, as Wrigley and Schofield establish it, was 32.4 years. By the 1820s it was 38.7 years.[3] So life had lengthened and mortality declined by a bit more than six years on average from the start of the period until the end. But Wrigley and Schofield can demonstrate mathematically that a rise in fertility, which occurred during the same period, contributed two and a half times as much to the outcome of population increase as did the decline in mortality, substantial as that was.[4]

The chief cause, then, of the increase in population in England during the long eighteenth century was a rise in fertility; and this rise was realized, as Wrigley and Schofield show, in several different ways. First of all, more women got married. At the start of the period, about 15 percent of all women who survived through the years of their fertility never married. By the end of the period, no more than half that percentage of all women who survived through the years of their fertility never married. This drop in the percentage of single women seems to have occurred mostly in the latter part of the eighteenth century.[5] Second, the average age of the first marriage for men as well as women fell by about three years, from twenty-six to twenty-three. This drop in the age of first marriage seems also to have occurred mostly during the latter part of the eighteenth century.[6] Finally, there was a marked increase in the rate of illegitimate births. At the start of the period only about 2 percent of all births were illegitimate. At the end of the period it was about

8 percent. This rise in the illegitimacy rate is more important than the figures may suggest. Another way of expressing the same rise, a way that may make its importance plainer, is that at the start of the period less than one-tenth of all first births were illegitimate but that at the end of the period about a quarter were.[7] I should add that an additional quarter were legitimate but prenuptially conceived and that this figure, too, represented a marked increase.[8] Like the drop in average age of first marriage, like the increase in the percentage of women marrying, the rise in illegitimacy and in prenuptial pregnancy seems to have occurred mostly during the latter part of the century.

To sum up, a rise in fertility was realized in these ways: more women got married than had done before, women and men married earlier in their lives than they had done before, and women had more illegitimate children and prenuptial pregnancies than they had done before. Chiefly because of the resultant rise in fertility,[9] and only very secondarily because of a concurrent decline in mortality, England's population grew from 4.93 million to 13.28 million in the course of about 150 years, but with special acceleration during the latter part of the eighteenth century.

What all this means is that there was a remarkable increase in the *incidence* of cross-sex genital intercourse (penis in vagina, vagina around penis, with seminal emission uninterrupted) during the late eighteenth century in England. I mean that this particular kind of sexual expression, which we moderns often tendentiously name "sexual intercourse," became more popular at that time in England, so much more popular that by means of that enhanced popularity alone, without any assistance from a decline in mortality, England's population could have doubled in a relatively short span. With the assistance of a decline in mortality, the population actually more than doubled.

That is my deduction from the demographic data—that sexual intercourse so-called became importantly more popular in late eighteenth-century England—and I believe that the deduction is irresistible. It is, however, a deduction that the demographers do not make. They do not say it; they do not seem to see it. I should guess that for all of us, whether or not we are demographers, seeing, saying, deducing such propositions on the history of sexual behavior may be peculiarly difficult. It isn't primarily a matter of embarrassment, of a fear of indecorum, though embarrassment and fear may, of course, play a part in restraining some of us. It's more a matter of a very strong feeling we're likely to have that such deductions and observations are, first, too bizarre to be cogent, yet, second, too obvious to be worth seeing and saying. We can easily feel both ways simultaneously. On some other occasion I should like to say more about that discomfiting dual feeling. For now, I want to remark that in my opinion the feeling is ideologically determined, and that in the measure we give way to it and allow it to govern us we reinforce that essentialism that so disempowers us both as historians and as political beings.

If we take seriously the deduction I've put to you, then many lines of inquiry open before us. We may, for instance, want to ask *why* sexual intercourse so-called should have become so much more popular in late eighteenth-century England. Nor need we be deterred from asking that question by our realization that we don't in the least know how to go about answering it, that we don't even know what would constitute an adequate answer to it. By permitting ourselves to ask it, we may eventually learn how to answer it. We may also want to ask whether or not this change in sexual practice is related to any change in late eighteenth-century English conceptions of what sex is, what it is for.

Returning for the moment to the demographers, we may note that although they don't make the deduction I've put to you nor ask the questions I've just asked, they do try to account for their data by asking another question: why did people marry earlier in life and why did more women marry?[10] One worrisome disadvantage to this question is that it doesn't save the appearances, that it doesn't fully respond to the data on fertility that the authors themselves present. Their data show not only a fall in the average age of marriage partners at first marriage, with consequences for population, but also a rise in the rate of illegitimacy and prenuptial conception, with consequences for population—that is to say, their data show more sexual intercourse so-called both inside and outside marriage. On the other hand, their question has also a certain advantage. Even if answering the question couldn't explain what needs explaining, the question is at least comfortable. The demographers imagine that they know, and maybe most of us would imagine that we know, how to go about trying to provide an answer for a question such as theirs. When the point at issue is understood simply as earlier marrying and more marrying, then surely we would look almost automatically for a rise in the wage rate as the likely cause. The demographers do look for a rise in the wage rate, but to their obvious disappointment they cannot find the causal connection they expect. Wages go up, but they go up a good thirty years in advance of the fertility rate; and thirty years, as the demographers concede, is probably too long an interval to fit into a causal argument of the sort they want to make.[11] Still, their failure to answer the question they ask is less remarkable than their evasion of their own data with that question. What they do is defensively transform something that ought to be a problem in the history of sexual behavior into a problem in the history of nuptiality so that they can proceed comfortably, if unsuccessfully.

I'd like to suggest that the conclusion I've deduced from the demographers' data, that sexual intercourse so-called came to be importantly more popular in late eighteenth-century England, may be related to another contemporary experience. The new popularity of intercourse so-called doesn't follow from, or depend on, a rise in wages; and it is only when we misunderstand the data as simply about marrying that we are tempted even to look to wage rates for an explanation. But the new popularity of intercourse so-called does correlate rather well with a dramatic rise in virtually all indices of production, a rise that the textbooks call the onset of the Industrial Revolution and that, as we know, distinguished late eighteenth-century England. I don't mean to imply that this rise in production, which was probably the biggest since the invention of agriculture in prehistoric times, caused the rise in intercourse so-called, nor do I mean to imply that the rise in intercourse so-called caused the rise in production. Neither of these causal arguments seems sound to me, and both would of course depend on a too easy and conventional distinction between the sexual and material realms. What does seem to me at least conceivable, though I am just speculating in saying so, is that the rise in production (the privileging of production) and the rise in the popularity of the sexual act that uniquely makes for reproduction (the privileging of intercourse so-called) may be aspects of the same phenomenon. Viewed from different perspectives, this phenomenon could be called either capitalism or the discourse of capitalism or modern heterosexuality or the discourse of modern heterosexuality.

It is of course true that sexual intercourse so-called had been valued in some measure or another, on some grounds or another, before the late eighteenth century and in every previous European society about which we know anything. But it is also true that production had been valued before the late eighteenth century in every previous European society about which we know anything. What happens to production in the late eighteenth century in England is nevertheless new. While production increased significantly, it also became discursively and phenomenologically central in ways that it had never been before. Behaviors, customs, usages that were judged to be nonproductive, like the traditional plebeian conception of time, according to which Mondays and maybe Tuesdays and Wednesdays as well are free days, play days, rest days ("St. Monday" was the plebeian phrase), came under extraordinary and ever-intensifying negative pressure.[12] If I should be right in speculating that the rise in popularity of sexual intercourse so-called in late eighteenth-century England is an aspect of the same phenomenon that includes the rise in production, then we should expect to find that sexual intercourse so-called becomes at this time and in this place discursively and phenomenologically central in ways that it had never been before, that nonreproductive sexual behaviors come under extraordinary negative pressure, and finally that both developments happen in ways that testify to their relatedness, even to their unity.

I cannot say that I have such findings to present to you. As I mentioned before, I am just at a speculative beginning. But I can say something about where my attention is currently directed. The earlier part of the long eighteenth century, before the big rise in production and in the incidence of sexual intercourse so-called, was an era of relatively late marriage, low illegitimacy and pre-nuptial pregnancy rates, and a relatively high rate of nonmarrying for women. According to some students of plebeian sexuality, like Flandrin, Quaife, and Bray, this was also an era of very diverse sexual practice. If outside of marriage plebeians typically avoided sexual intercourse so-called (penis in vagina, vagina around penis, with seminal emission uninterrupted), they were nevertheless typically sexually active. They practiced mutual masturbation, oral sex, anal sex, display and watching (or to use the more common and pejorative terms, "exhibitionism" and "voyeurism"), and much else besides, on a cross-sex basis and in some now uncertain measure on a same-sex basis as well.[13]

What happens to the tradition of same-sex sexual behaviors in the late eighteenth century is something that I shall put aside for now. It is an intricate problem and demands extended and separate treatment. As for what happens to the tradition of very diverse cross-sex sexual behaviors, my hypothesis is: they are reorganized and reconstructed in the late eighteenth century as foreplay. They don't disappear, they aren't ruled out, as the incidence of intercourse so-called increases, but they are relegated and largely confined to the position of the preliminary. From the late eighteenth century on, they are construed as what precedes that sexual behavior that alone is privileged, intercourse so-called. On this hypothesis, the invention of foreplay—an important passage in the making of modern heterosexuality—is to be understood as homologous with the crowding of St. Monday, Tuesday, and Wednesday into Sunday, the first day of the work week—an important passage in the making of capitalism. Rest doesn't disappear, isn't ruled out, as production rises, but rest is relegated and largely confined to the position of the preliminary. To put it differently, I hypothesize that the invention of foreplay is an aspect of the history of capitalism, that the invention of industrial work-discipline is an aspect of the history of heterosexuality, and that both developments are in an important sense the same.

From Thoreau to Queer Politics

Henry David Thoreau's *Walden* was first published at the beginning of August 1854, and it was immediately and relatively widely reviewed in the United States periodical press. On August 9, the *Boston Daily Bee* called *Walden* an "original book" and its author "very eccentric." On August 10, the *Boston Daily Journal* called it a "remarkable" book and its author "eccentric." On August 12, the *New Bedford (Mass.) Mercury* repeated the judgment of Thoreau as "eccentric." On September 22, the *New York Times* referred to the author's "eccentricities" without specifying them. On October 4, *Putnam's Monthly Magazine* called Thoreau a *"lusus,"* a sport. On October 28, the *Yankee Blade* said that he had "an odd twist in his brains," while the *Knickerbocker,* in its review, published rather late in March of the year following, repeated the more usual term of coded description, "eccentric." If the author of *Walden* was describable, then, as eccentric, or as very eccentric, or as a sport, or even as having an odd twist in his brains, who, as his reviewers saw it, were likely to be his readers? The *Daily Alta California,* of October 8, answered this question in its review by recommending *Walden* "to all fops, male and female" both.[1]

Along with these vague but somehow pointed descriptions of author and potential readers, there was usually also a negative moral judgment on the book. "Selfish" was the favored term of disapprobation. The *Boston Daily Journal* said that *Walden* described a "selfish existence" and conveyed "selfish opinions" and propounded a "selfish philosophy." The *Morning Courier* and the *New-York Enquirer* said that the book was "repulsively selfish," and the *New York Times* said that the book had a "selfish animus."[2]

Nor is there any difficulty in determining what exactly the first reviewers thought was selfish in *Walden*. On this matter the *Boston Atlas* was particularly forceful and explicit. It pointed out, with some considerable show of indignation, that the author had not, even in his imagination, peopled his hut at the pond "with a loving and beloved wife and blooming children." The *Atlas* added that there was not one word in all of *Walden* about "woman's" love, "pure, constant" and "suffering." The *National Era* was as indignant as the *Atlas*. It argued that for American men to follow Thoreau's selfish example would be first of all impossible but second of all disastrous. If men should try, then how long, the *National Era* asked rhetorically, "would they remain civilized, by squatting upon solitary duck-ponds, eschewing matrimony" and "casting off all ties of family?" The *New York Churchman* further elaborated on this theme of marriage and family by suggesting that Thoreau was mistaken to suppose that the mass of men were discontented. On the contrary, the typical American countryman, however dull and deadening his workday might be, still had a cardinal advantage that the selfish Thoreau lacked: "the treasures" of wife and children. Finally, the periodical *Graham's,* in developing the usual theme of selfishness in its review of *Walden,* actually said of Thoreau that he had gone "beyond" the "come-outers."[3]

Eccentric, twisted in his brains, maybe a sport, selfish, maybe even repulsively selfish because of his life without marriage, the love of woman, and children, because of his life without even wistfully imagining marriage, the love of woman, and children: that was the way the Thoreau figured in *Walden* was first interpreted in the American periodical press. But by the time of Thoreau's death in 1862, just eight years after *Walden* had been published and first reviewed, vigorous efforts were underway to provide a less condemnatory, less indignant, and less insinuating reading of both the author and the book. No one contributed more prominently to these vigorous reclamatory efforts than Thoreau's fellow townsman, Ralph Waldo Emerson. In the eulogy he spoke at Concord immediately after Thoreau's death and later published in the *Atlantic Monthly*, Emerson tried hard to obviate the impression left by the first reviews and to place Thoreau firmly and finally in the pantheon of American polite culture. To place him there, Emerson had to reassure those of his readers who were disturbed by what they had already read about Thoreau. In reassuring them, Emerson faced what presumably he took to be their main concern head-on. He acknowledged to his readers that many young men had gathered around Thoreau. He said, "I have repeatedly known young men of sensibility converted in a moment to the belief that this was the man they were in search of, the man of men, who could tell them all they should do." However, Emerson added, Thoreau's "dealing with" these young men had never been "affectionate, but" rather "superior, didactic." After providing this reassurance on the main point along with assorted reminiscences and passages of elegiac praise, Emerson went on to a verbally splendid finale in which he compared Thoreau's life and work to the search occasionally undertaken by Swiss hunters for the rare Alpine flower edelweiss, which, Emerson explained, signified "Noble Purity." "There is a flower," Emerson said,

> which grows on the most inaccessible cliffs of the Tyrolese mountains . . . , and which the hunter, tempted by its beauty, and by his love (for it is immensely valued by the Swiss maidens), climbs the cliffs to gather, and is sometimes found dead at the foot, with the flower in his hand. . . . Thoreau seemed to me living in the hope to gather this plant, which belonged to him as of right.[4]

With that finale, Emerson completed his contribution to the task of reclamation. And the contribution was considerable. He had assimilated Thoreau to the grand narrative of connubiality, the narrative that I suppose most of us still live by and that Thoreau had previously been thought to be disrupting. In Emerson's tribute, Thoreau was no longer the eccentric, the sport, the twisted one who lived selfishly without marriage, the love of woman, and children. Thoreau was rather the brave and hardy seeker, whose life and work were devoted to the search for the ideal gift of courtship for the nameless maiden representing all that was fair and whose love he hoped to deserve. While seeking that gift, that flower, that noble purity, Thoreau was never affectionate to young men.

I should hazard the opinion that on the whole Emerson's reading of Thoreau—perhaps I should say rather his domestication of Thoreau—has prevailed from the 1860s until now. Relatively few are still interested in the disruptive figure who was seen in *Walden* by its first reviewers, the figure who went "beyond" the "come-outers."

I spent a year of sabbatical in 1991–92 in Salt Lake City, Utah, where I belonged to the local chapter of Queer Nation. I should explain that I did not belong to Queer Nation so that I could write about it. I was not an observer there, nor even a participant-observer, but rather a full-fledged and committed member. Our group was small—there was a core of about a dozen regulars—but very busy, close, and intimate. Every week we met once all together for a planning meeting, usually once more all together to do an "action," usually again all together to go to a movie and have dinner at our favorite Greek diner, and once in a three- or four-person focus group. Each such focus group had a project of its own. For instance, one of them produced a magazine called *Queer Fuckers Magazine*. There were two issues during the year I was in Utah.

Our membership was about half men, half women, mostly white, partly Latina, and except for me and one other, all ex-Mormon. On the whole the local lesbian/gay community looked askance at us; we were the extremists. Nevertheless, we were permitted to hold our meetings in the local lesbian/gay community center, the Stonewall Center. Some care, I think, was taken by the Center's board to schedule our weekly planning meeting on an evening different from that allocated for the meeting of the Mormon lesbian/gay group, Affirmation. Relations between Queer Nation and Affirmation were, as you might suppose, particularly shaky.

While I was part of Queer Nation/Salt Lake City, I tried to think about the kind of group it was, the kind of politics it practiced, whether or not they were really good politics, and how if at all they were new politics. I had been involved in many other political groups before, even in many other lesbian/gay political groups, and there were, I thought, some features of Queer Nation/Salt Lake City, possibly of all the other chapters of Queer Nation, that were certainly noteworthy and maybe new as well. For one thing and most obviously, there was the privileging of the term "queer," a term that has none of the supposititious definiteness of "lesbian," "bisexual," or "gay." Just what "queer" signifies or includes or refers to is by no means easy to say.[5] Yet we almost always called ourselves queer, and we let the more familiar terms go by the board. Then there was the commitment to visibility mixed with outrage and humor. Wherever we went all together, whether to a meeting, an action, a dinner, or a movie, we were festooned in queer regalia, buttons, signs, and illustrated T-shirts. I usually wore a sign with just these words: "Elder Queer." Sometimes we also chanted. For instance, a small contingent traveled to Los Angeles for the big Academy Awards celebration. These queers stood, festooned as usual, just outside the auditorium where the celebration was to be held, and chanted as the celebrities arrived, "We're here, we're queer, we're fabulous, and we designed everything that you're wearing!"

Some other features of Queer Nation/Salt Lake City also seemed striking. There was relatively little interest in lesbian/gay civil rights issues, such as domestic partnership legislation or those antidiscrimination bills now passed in scores of municipalities and several states, bills that provide some limited protection for lesbian, gay, and bisexual people in the housing, credit, and employment markets. On the other hand, there was keen and lively interest in producing actions in response to homophobic incidents. For instance, a radio talk-show host was notorious for his homophobic backchat. We made zestful, loud, and peculiar scenes outside a store in which he had a financial stake. Or another example, the manager of a local fast-food place kicked out two lesbians who had kissed one another while in a line waiting to be shown to a table. A week later we arrived at this fast-food place in force, about thirty of us, got safely seated in small groups all over the restaurant, and then simultaneously started kissing at some dozen separate tables. The manager, running frantically from table to table, ordered us all to leave, but we refused and kissed on. These were actions. And finally, another feature that seemed striking was our interest in the concept and rhetoric of nationhood, an interest that was apparent in the very name of our organization, a name that indubitably produced much satisfaction for the members.

I thought about these striking and in some ways puzzling features—the privileging of the term "queer," the emphasis on visibility, the relative lack of interest in civil rights issues, the commitment to actions, the preference for the language of nationhood—and in the intervals of other employment I developed some tentative and preliminary ideas about the genealogy and phenomenology of the new queer politics that Queer Nation/Salt Lake City exemplified. In this brief essay I want to focus on just two of these features—the concept of an action and the preference for the language of nationhood. My questions are: What is an action, in contradistinction to a demonstration or a protest or a picket? And second, why is there a nation in the name Queer Nation? Trying to answer these questions, I found myself, and still now find myself, referring often to *Walden*. In some moods I have almost wanted to say that the production of *Walden* was the first queer action.

Just why Thoreau should have built a cabin in the Concord woods near Walden Pond, a mile from the nearest neighbor, and remained there for twenty-six months has long been much disputed, and the book opens the way to the dispute since it is markedly vague on this very point. The site at the pond, the book says, "offers advantages which it may not be good policy to divulge."[6] On the other hand, just why Thoreau should have occasionally left his cabin and gone to visit the more populated parts of Concord has been much less disputed, presumably because so many of *Walden*'s readers have believed that the pull of the more populated parts needed no explaining. On this matter, however, the book does offer an explicit explanation: "I went," Thoreau says, "to see the men and boys."[7]

While he is at the pond, Thoreau himself receives visitors. Many people come to see him, and the visitor about whom he has the most to say is a French-Canadian woodchopper. Thoreau never mentions the woodchopper's name, but there is an extended description of his looks. No other person who appears in *Walden* is so extensively described: "He was about twenty-eight years old and cast," Thoreau tells us, "in the coarsest mold; a stout but sluggish body, yet gracefully carried, with a thick sun-burnt neck, dark bushy hair, and dull sleepy blue eyes. He wore a flat gray cloth cap, a dingy wool-colored great coat, and cowhide boots." "A more simple, natural man," Thoreau also says, "it would be hard to find."[8] He adds that the woodchopper was undeveloped intellectually and woefully undereducated.

Yet when the woodchopper comes to the cabin to visit, Thoreau takes out his Greek Homer and the two men then read in it together. No other scene of collaborative reading appears in *Walden*. The woodchopper, Thoreau explains, has been taught just enough Greek by his parish priest back home in Canada to be able to pronounce the letters. With the priest, the woodchopper had read aloud the sounds of the New Testament. With Thoreau it is not the testament; it is instead the *Iliad*. Thoreau gives him the book to hold and directs him to the passage where Achilles reproves Patroclus for his sad countenance. The woodchopper articulates the sounds, and then Thoreau translates for him:

Why are you in tears, Patroclus, like a young girl?
Or have you alone heard some news from Phthia?
They say that Menoetius lives yet, son of Actor
And Peleus lives, son of Aecus, among the Myrmidons,
Either of whom having died, we should greatly grieve.

After hearing this translation, the woodchopper, Thoreau says, replies simply, "That's good."[9]

This passage is, of course, a representation of seduction. Thoreau is figured as the seducer. He has the very Greek book. He puts it into the young man's hands, while they are secluded together at a remote cabin in the woods. The young man is figured as the object of the seduction. He knows at least the letters of this strange alphabet, he takes the book, and he sounds them aloud. He is natural and present, and he registers satisfaction when he learns what his sounds mean. As for the reading the two of them share, it is highly suggestive. For according to a famous and long-standing tradition of interpretation, Achilles was the lover of Patroclus.[10]

As a representation of seduction, the passage is extraordinary. What is perhaps still more extraordinary is the way in which the passage so fully mirrors Thoreau's relation to the readers of *Walden*. Throughout *Walden* Thoreau repeatedly asks his readers the same question that he translates from Homer for the woodchopper: Why so unnecessarily sad? Why so unnecessarily discontented? Just as Thoreau tries to arouse the woodchopper, so he tries to arouse his readers to what he again and again calls "life." Just as he hands the woodchopper a book, so he does to his readers, and as readers we are therefore all positioned, regardless of our gender or sexual taste, as the objects of a homosexual seduction. In addition, the more successfully we are enabled to read *Walden*, that is, the farther we get beyond just sounding the letters, the more willing we show ourselves.

I have been referring to Thoreau, and what I mean is Thoreau as he is represented in *Walden*. Ordinarily he is figured there as the first person, the narrator, the "I" who hands the book to the woodchopper. But Thoreau isn't only that I. There are also other ways that he is figured. In all of these, however, he is the seducer, the arouser, the awakener. For instance, Thoreau is chanticleer in the book's epigraph, an epigraph that is repeated word for word in the text itself: "I do not propose to write an ode to dejection, but to brag as lustily as chanticleer in the morning, standing on his roost, if only to wake his neighbors up."[11] Thoreau is also the "wood-nymph" in the chapter on "Sounds." He is "the true husband-man" in the chapter on "The Bean-Field." He is the fisher of men in the chapter on "The Ponds." Whether as lusty cock, as wood nymph, as true husbandman, or as fisher of men, he always leads us on.

But to what? What is this vivid life he brags of? I do not intend to provide a nuanced and fully developed answer to that question here. I want just to indicate, if only schematically, what I think should be fundamental to such an answer. What *Walden* figures as valuable and vivid is life outside the discourses of domesticity, romantic love and marriage, and the white bourgeois family. All these discourses are at least in the aspirations of the book left behind. To transcend them is *Walden*'s object, and if it fails fully to accomplish this transcending, the object remains.

I should further say that a particularly cogent way to appreciate *Walden*'s object is to see the book as an antinovel. It is in contradistinction to the novel format that *Walden* is realized. You may recall, if you are devoted novel readers as I am, that Moll Flanders, early in the novel that bears her name, reports that everyone in her neighborhood is "addicted to Family News."[12] But *Walden*, unlike Moll's novel or the general run of novels known in the 1850s, tells of no family news, no marriages, no engagements, no elopements, no inheritances, no births, no fraternal rivalries, no sororal solidarities. It remarks on none past, and it imagines none future. It features no house, just a nearly empty cabin, and it has no love interest. In fact, the ideal of love is as firmly rejected in *Walden* as are also the ideals of fame, money, and compassion.

That readers will certainly expect family news, and will be bored when they find it missing, Thoreau freely acknowledges. Commenting on the absence of domestic sounds in the woods, he says, "An old-fashioned man would have lost his senses or died of ennui before this."[13] *Walden* has several different ways of dealing with the disappointment and ennui it expects readers to feel as they read it, readers who are after all habituated to, or maybe as Moll says, even addicted to, family news. One way is to attack the novel as a genre, for the novel has been so important in helping to produce this habituation or addiction, and all novel readers as well. In one of the bitterest passages in *Walden*, Thoreau says that novel readers

> read the 9000th tale about Zebulon and Sephronia, and how they loved as none had ever loved before, and neither did the course of their true love run smooth—or at any rate how it did run and stumble, and get up again and go on! how some poor unfortunate got up into a steeple, who had better never have gone up as far as the belfry; and then, having needlessly got him up there, the happy novelist rings the bell for all the world to come together and hear, O dear! how he did get down again!

"For my part," Thoreau continues, "I think they had better metamorphose all such aspiring heroes of universal noveldom into man weathercocks, as they used to put heroes among the constellations, and let them swing round till they are rusty, and not come down to bother honest men with their pranks. The next time the novelist rings the bell I will not stir though the meeting-house burn down."[14] I won't comment in detail on this tirade, though it is well worth intensive scrutiny. I shall only point out Thoreau's remark that the male heroes of novels may as well be man weathercocks— in other words, chanticleer domesticated. If chanticleer, or the lusty cock, arouses, all that the novel hero can do is tell which way the wind is blowing.

I quote this at length to demonstrate the measure of *Walden*'s animus against the novels to which it is opposed. Along with the attack on novels and novel readers, *Walden* has other, perhaps more important ways of trying to reverse the boredom it expects to produce. It works hard, for instance, to represent interest and excitement in sites apart from domesticity, love, marriage, and family. It also provides its readers with a renovated sense of nation to take the place of that family that it has endeavored wholly to banish.

All readers of *Walden* are likely to remember Thoreau's brash confidence in moving into his cabin on the Fourth of July, as though to begin anew what the old Puritans had called the errand into the wilderness, as though the weight and import of his project somehow entitled him to do America all over again. But just as crucial as the brashness, as the confidence, of the famous Fourth of July gesture is the measure of Thoreau's identification with the nation, an identification to which the gesture witnesses. His project and the nation's would seem, in his view, to be the same. Although he is often figured as alone in *Walden,* his basic political stance is nevertheless in some crucial sense collectivist. "To act collectively," Thoreau says in *Walden,* "is according to the spirit of our institutions,"[15] and the collectivity he depends on most, for legitimation, for inspiration, for a forum for his cultural production, is the nation. I should, however, add that Thoreau represents himself as despising the American state quite as much as he requires the American nation.

Perhaps we may now return to Queer Nation/Salt Lake City and to the two questions I advanced earlier about the new queer politics. I asked first, what is an action, in contradistinction to a demonstration or a protest or a picket? And second, why is there a nation in the name Queer Nation? I don't know that I can answer these questions, but I hope at least to comment on them helpfully.

Like a demonstration or a protest or a picket, an action is a way of trying to do what is thought by the doers to be in the circumstances politically salient. Unlike a demonstration or a protest or a picket, or at least much more than these, an action expresses a felt need to create a wholly nondomestic site of excitement, outrage, and interest. An action is, structurally speaking, a response to an experience or expectation of ennui, an ennui that is culturally produced by the absence in queer life or aspiration of those family excitements and interests to which we are all, queer or not, required to be habituated. I should perhaps add that in my opinion the creation of such nondomestic sites of excitement, outrage, and interest is something of great value. But there is more to be said to distinguish and explain the action as a form of doing.

When formerly, before the days of queer politics, we made just demonstrations, say as part of a campaign for a lesbian/gay civil rights bill, we were, I think, in fact demonstrating something. What we were demonstrating was a conviction, a conviction that a lesbian/gay civil rights bill was proper and necessary, that we lesbians and gay men were marginalized in American society and needed protection against discrimination. Similarly, when in the 1960s we demonstrated against the U.S. military adventure in Vietnam, we were also demonstrating a conviction, a conviction that this military adventure was wrong. An action, on the other hand, always puts forward a claim that is not yet quite a conviction. If we say, "We're here, we're queer, we're fabulous, and we designed everything that you're wearing," then we assert not our marginalization but rather our centrality. This claim, as we nowadays may make it, is less than a conviction but more, I should say, than just a hope. To make the claim requires a performance rather than a demonstration. It requires that we be actorish.

I am reminded of Paul Goodman's extraordinarily prescient essay of 1969, "The Politics of Being Queer." In that essay, Goodman says, "I act that 'the society I live in is mine.'"[16] An action, then, if I may summarize, is a way of trying to do what is politically salient while countering, often sensationally, the ennui produced by the disruption of the discourses of family, love, and marriage, and while also performing or acting a claim to centrality.

I said before that we who are queer do not yet fully believe our own claims to centrality. That is my impression. But I think that we should try to believe them. They are at least as cogent as are our more familiar claims to marginalization. As one bit of evidence of queer centrality and power in these provinces, particularly in the culture of these provinces, I offer *Walden*. And what of the name Queer Nation? I do not think that the signification of this name is as mysterious and difficult as most commentators on the subject have assumed. What Queer Nation really means is America.

The Queering of Lesbian/Gay History

By now the bibliography of books and articles on lesbian and gay history is large, and it is rapidly growing larger. I won't try to comment in this essay on that entire bibliography. Instead, I'll limit myself to just some of the English-language writing produced since the 1960s and concerned specifically with the emergence of lesbian and gay identity, community, and culture in the modern era. My object is to say something about a body of historical writing and about my students as well—my current undergraduate students, most of whom are U.S. Americans like me, but a full generation younger than I am—and about the response of these students to that body of writing.

I should explain that, because of a series of happy accidents, I have been placed for nearly the whole of my teaching career at Wesleyan, a university that attracts large numbers of out and politically active students. In years gone by, many of these students called themselves "lesbian" and "gay." I have shared a classroom with more than a thousand such students. During the last five years the terms "lesbian" and "gay" have become relatively less appealing to the undergraduates at our university, and many of them have lately preferred to call themselves "queer." I have now shared a classroom with hundreds of queer students. I do not believe that this change is only—or even primarily—in nomenclature. It seems more consequential than that. I should characterize it as very fundamental indeed, a change that amounts to a shift in sensibility, style, tone, values, and commitments. For one thing, this change has apparently produced a partly new way of reading and thinking history. When my queer students read the major English-language works of lesbian/gay history published since the late 1960s and dealing with the modern emergence of lesbian and gay identity, community, and culture, they respond to this work differently than did their lesbian and gay predecessors of just a very few years ago in the same classroom.

As a teacher, I usually find myself expounding a body of history writing. Here I want to try to expound both such a body of writing and my current undergraduate students' response to it. To put it another way, I'm going to treat my students as "an interpretive community" and then interpret them interpreting history.[1] In this project there are, of course, risks and built-in weaknesses. Most obviously, there is the risk that I may misrepresent or misrecognize these students. They and I work together and know one another reasonably well, but we aren't the same. My formation was as a gay man, not as a queer, and about their queerness, its consequences, and its implications, I might easily be mistaken. Furthermore, my observations are of these students in interaction with me as teacher, and my presence as teacher is bound to affect what I observe. For instance, I have a commitment to the theory-based critique of history writing. My students know of this commitment. They may feel greater license to do such critical work in my presence than in other places or circumstances. They may even feel obliged to do such work in my presence! And, as I plan to show, they do lots of it. Finally, my conclusions are based on a very limited sample of queers—all of them students and at only one university. They may or may not be typical of queers elsewhere.

One of my most dependable resources as a teacher of modern lesbian and gay history is the excellent anthology *Hidden from History*, edited by Martin Duberman, Martha Vicinus, and George Chauncey Jr., and published in 1989, just before the rise of the queers. I want to draw attention to a passage in the editors' introduction because this passage may serve as a point of entry to much of the rest of what I plan to say. Here, the key word for my purposes is "marginalization." In the very first paragraph of the introduction the editors declare, "Repression and marginalization have often been the lot of historians of homosexuality as well as of homosexuals themselves."[2] Although they go on to show that by 1989 "historians of homosexuality" had become less marginal professionally than they had been previously, the editors still convey the view that in the past lesbian and gay people had been marginalized and that in more recent times lesbian and gay people, and their historians too, have been just less marginalized.

If these editors record the marginalization of lesbian and gay people in the past, then so do most of the other English-language history writers who since the late 1960s have published on the modern emergence of lesbian and gay identity, community, and culture. Take Jeffrey Weeks. In his important and pioneering 1977 book, *Coming Out*, a history of homosexual politics in Great Britain from the late nineteenth century until his own time, Weeks focuses largely on the struggle for the reform of laws penalizing homosexual behaviors, and he characterizes the reformers as emerging from an originally secret, later bravely open, but continuously marginalized lesbian and gay subculture.[3] Or take Carroll Smith-Rosenberg's illuminating study of the development of the "New Woman" in the United States from the 1870s to the 1930s. At the beginning of the study, and in a way that inflects the whole of her argument, Smith-Rosenberg describes the "New Woman" and her "discursive strategy" as an instance of the struggle of "the marginal" and "powerless" against "the dominant" and "hegemonical."[4] Or take John D'Emilio's thoughtful and deeply researched 1983 book, *Sexual Politics, Sexual Communities: The Making of a Homosexual Minority in the United States, 1940–1970*. D'Emilio tells the story of the U.S. homophile movement of the 1950s and 1960s. He sees this movement as arising in an urban "sexual subculture," then as acting through political, organizational, and cultural work to transform that marginal "subculture" into an "urban community."[5] Or take Lillian Faderman's 1991 survey, *Odd Girls and Twilight Lovers: A History of Lesbian Life in Twentieth-Century America.* In her epilogue, Faderman sums up her chronological account of U.S. American lesbianism this way: lesbianism, she says, has been transformed in the twentieth century "from a state from which most women who loved women dissociated themselves, to a secret and often lonely acknowledgment that one fell into that 'category,' to groups of women who formed a subculture around the concept, to a sociopolitical statement and a civil rights movement that claimed its own minority status and even formed its own ghettos."[6] Although Faderman doesn't use the word "marginalization" in this passage, her summary descriptions of the stages in the development of twentieth-century lesbianism all connote marginalization. These various works of history are different from one another in many ways, but each, I think, makes important use of the trope of marginalization.

I don't want to seem to be suggesting that my current queer undergrads reject this history of marginalized peoples struggling, that they find this history wrong. They don't reject it, and they don't find it wrong. But they also don't own it in anything like the same measure as did their lesbian and gay predecessors at our university. For they do not typically experience their own subjectivity as marginal, even at those moments when they feel most oppressed by homophobic and heterosexist discourses and institutions. Marginalization isn't their preferred trope. It doesn't seem to them to be cogent as a narrative device for organizing the telling of their own lives or, for that matter, of their history. What these queers prefer to say and believe or try to believe instead is that they are both present and at the center. This, I think, is what they probably mean by their repeated and emphatic use of the word "here." "We are here," arguably the most famous of all queer chants, is very different from the old lesbian/gay liberation slogan of the 1970s, "We are everywhere." That slogan was chiefly valued as thrilling, and in my experience it was always understood as hyperbolic as well. But "we are here" isn't in the least hyperbolic, and I believe it may be heard, even by its speakers, as more demanding and threatening than thrilling. I note, for instance, that the undergrad queers at a university near mine have tried to make the demanding and threatening character of their queerness explicit by titling their community news bulletin "In Your Faces." But this title is just a rhetorically inflated version of "We are here."

When I say that these queers don't care much for the trope of marginalization and prefer to represent themselves as present and central, even threateningly so, I should add that for them presence and centrality don't connote mainstreamism or assimilation. They don't typically see themselves as inside what the historian Arthur Schlesinger Jr. called "the vital center."[7] By that phrase Schlesinger meant the nonreactionary and nonradical citizenry whom he be-lieved to be—I think wrongly—the best hope of democracy. On the contrary, these queers typically see themselves as radical. Nor for them do presence and centrality mean dominativeness, power. They know quite well that their power is limited, that they aren't in any crucial sense dominative in U.S. American society. If they nevertheless feel committed to the trope of presence and centrali-ty, they probably understand centrality roughly as Emerson did when he said that the "artist" was "central" in her or his society. I believe that they may think this way, even though they certainly never quote Emerson. I should add that these queers typically see themselves as in a sense similar to artists, performance artists espe-cially, and that they slide into or toward performance in almost all circumstances.

Are these queer students, you may be wondering, mostly of one gender, one race, one class? They certainly aren't of one gender. I have not done a quantitative study, but I should say that there are probably more women than men among them, though only by a small percentage. Racially and ethnically they are very mixed. In class origins, on the other hand, they are relatively uniform. Our university is expensive, and these queer students tend to be mostly well-off and bourgeois. So, too, were their lesbian and gay predecessors. I doubt that these students' queerness is a class-determined phenomenon, any more than their predecessors' lesbianism and gayness were. What I do think likely is that their class position may help them to be confident in the expression of their queerness in the classroom.

When I teach these queers the historical narratives that describe lesbian and gay struggle from sites of marginalization, they are by no means unappreciative of the narratives. And as I said before, they do not reject them as wrong. Still, they are critical in two different ways. First, they press me hard, as the sole representative in the classroom of the generation of historians who wrote the narratives, on whether marginalization was really always immanent in the historical record. What I think they suspect is that we older historians need the trope of marginalization, project it onto everything, use it obsessively, and that this trope is somehow weak, even when it produces a story of struggle. If I reply that the homophile movement of the 1950s is probably best conceived as a struggle from the margin, and that this struggle may have helped to usher in a world in which they could feel less marginal than their forbears, they aren't especially impressed, much less persuaded. For they also have a second line of criticism. Focus elsewhere, they say. Don't focus on histories that require the trope of marginalization for their telling. Let those histories of marginality be marginal. If the history of the homophile movement has to be a story of struggling from the margin, then turn partly away from it. Focus on the musical comedies of the 1950s. What could be queerer? Or focus on the popular movies of the lesbian film director Dorothy Arzner and their reception. Or go back some years further and focus on the songs of Cole Porter.[8] All these cultural productions were central rather than marginal. By ignoring or neglecting them, we misconceive the past and unwittingly reduce our presence in and claim to the present, they say.

They have more to say, too. Just as they criticize the trope of marginalization, so they also criticize the way that human agency is figured in the history books about the emergence of lesbian and gay identity, community, and culture. For these queer students, the self is a myth, a delusion, a sham, a part of the ideology of humanism, and in their eyes humanism has long since been fundamentally and irrevocably discredited. I cannot say that they typically give what seems to me to be a good account of their reasons for their certainty that humanism and the self are both wrong and gone. Some of them have read extensively in Foucault, and virtually all of them have read at least a little in Foucault. But I believe that their position may derive less from that reading than from a body of assumptions, opinions, and dicta shared widely in, and absorbed readily from, the university world around them. In other words, they typically insist that the self is a retrograde concept without necessarily knowing how to say why. Along with the self, they also resist as misleading and destructive the concepts of originality and inner depth. As a result, they react with something ranging between boredom and incredulity to the representation in history books of persons with deep subjectivity and a capacity for original and decisive action.

Take again, for instance, Weeks's book, *Coming Out*. Weeks repeatedly comments on what he calls the "self-activity" of the Gay Liberation Front members in the early 1970s. By "self-activity" he means to provide a kind of portmanteau term for the members' vigorous efforts to think deeply and reflectively through their own oppression toward a strategy for struggling to overcome it—to make, to devise, and even to invent a consciousness and an identity based on pride that would sustain and nourish them in this struggle. Weeks mentions Aubrey Walter and Bob Mellors as two particularly influential members of Britain's Gay Liberation Front. Summing up the achievements of these two men and of the other members of the Front, Weeks writes, "Gay pride replaced self-oppression."[9] My queer students turn away from this quasi-heroic account of self-activity, for they don't really believe in selves, much less self-activity. Perhaps I can best clarify what I take to be the position of these students if I say that they typically find anonymity more interesting than individuality, imitation more believable than originality, and appropriation more desirable than invention. For instance, since about 1991 they have typically been great admirers of the San Francisco–based activist group Boy With Arms Akimbo. Boy's members are anonymous. What they do is reproduce, as posters, images of sex taken from many different sources—pulp novels, old sex education manuals, textbooks; sign the posters with their Boy logo; add a two-word caption, either "Sex is" or "Just sex"; and then wheatpaste the posters in public places all over San Francisco and other cities.[10] Boy's posters have probably amounted to an effective political intervention in a U.S. American context. But the students admire more than just Boy's effectiveness and militancy. They are also heartened by what they take to be Boy's disarticulation of individuality, by Boy's reliance on only appropriated images, and most of all by the flat, blasé, insouciant, antiromantic, and antihumanist rhetoric of Boy's captions, "Sex is" and "Just sex." "Why can't we have history with a tone like that of those captions?" one queer student asked me. This question, for which I had no ready answer, is indicative of what I take to be their outlook and primary commitments.[11] For if these students are bored, incredulous, about the representation in history books of persons with deep subjectivity and a capacity for original and decisive action, they are downright indignant when in their reading they find such persons represented as undergoing sexual liberation or as arriving at sexual authenticity.

If the queer students are sure of anything, it is that having sex doesn't liberate, however pleasurable it may be. This they have learned from some contemporary feminist theory and perhaps also from Foucault. In the students' view, sex isn't now— and can't have been in the past—an arena for liberation or for transcendence or for the achieving of authenticity. They say instead, following Boy With Arms Akimbo, "Sex is." Take, for instance, the fine study of lesbian bar culture in Buffalo, New York, during the 1940s and 1950s by Madeline Davis and Elizabeth Lapovsky Kennedy. This study has produced several articles and a book. I haven't yet had an opportunity to assign the whole book, but I have repeatedly assigned the Davis and Kennedy article printed in the Duberman, Vicinus,

Sex Is. Boy With Arms Akimbo, San Francisco, 1989.

and Chauncey anthology. The article focuses on butch-fem roles in
Buffalo bar culture. At one point Davis and Kennedy write, "butch-
fem roles created an authentic lesbian sexuality appropriate to the
flourishing of an independent lesbian culture."[12] This is the point at

which the queer students usually erupt. Let me make clear that they don't object to the account of butch-fem. Quite to the contrary, they typically approve and enjoy that aspect of the article, and the women, I believe, happily appropriate 1940s and 1950s butch-fem images and styles to their 1990s lives. What they object to is the concept of authenticity that Davis and Kennedy deploy. For the queer students think that there is not and cannot be such a thing as authenticity, and that there certainly is not and cannot be such a thing as an "authentic lesbian sexuality."

If these queer students were writing history books on their own, there would, I feel reasonably sure, be no representation in them of persons who find liberation or authenticity through sex, unless, of course, the representation was ironic or parodic. But would these students want to banish also any representation of persons with deep subjectivity and a capacity for original and decisive action? Yes, I think so. Perhaps I can clarify what I take to be their position if I say that they would prefer that, insofar as persons were to be represented in history books, the persons should be figured on the model of characters in late twentieth-century fiction rather than on the model of characters in mid-Victorian fiction. When I say characters in late twentieth-century fiction, I mean characters who have indefinite boundaries, who are always slipping in and out of focus, who are never fully constituted, never reliably whole, never coherent. I should also say that in the history the students would prefer to read, and one day may start to write, there would be simply fewer representations of individual persons of any sort than are to be found in the works of lesbian and gay history that I assign to them. Many of these students have had experience in literature and cultural studies courses in studying texts of all sorts—magazine stories, poems, films, television sitcoms; and they are familiar with the theoretical premise that such texts should be analyzed without reference to some supposititiously intentional author or authors. To read, even to write, the cultural history of texts such as these may be the students' ambition, and the type of cultural history they prefer would figure the text and its mass audience as a discursive field, a field from which historical agents or authors—persons in the familiar sense—were largely absent.

On one other matter as well these queer students typically resist the books and articles on the emergence of lesbian and gay identity, community, and culture that I assign to them. Many of these books and articles present their narratives in a national framework. For instance, Weeks's *Coming Out* focuses mostly on Great Britain, while Smith-Rosenberg's article on the "New Woman," Faderman's book on twentieth-century lesbianism, and D'Emilio's book on the homophile reformers focus mostly on the United States. I find the queer attitude toward the nation-state hard to sort out. So far as I can tell, the attitude is mixed. On the one hand, these students typically say that they would prefer historical narratives that weren't framed by the nation, narratives framed instead either by some subnational entity or by the globe. In their preference for local or transnational history, they would seem to be leery of the nation-state. On the other hand, they readily appropriate the language of nationalism for their political work. One of the earliest queer activist groups in the United States was called Queer Nation.[13] In their readiness to appropriate the language of nationalism, they would seem to be favorable to the nation-state. It is possible, of course, that they may be both leery and favorable simultaneously and ambivalently, as I suppose many others are on this same matter. But it is also possible that they may want to make a tacit distinction between narrative framing and appropriation, that they may consider narrative framing as more consequential and problematic than the appropriation of bits and pieces of lingo and iconography.

In any case, these queer students typically resist national history narratives. What they say is that citizenship in their own nation-state and in Great Britain, perhaps in other nation-states as well, is now, and has long been, constituted by exclusions based on race and class. Any narrative that assumes the nation-state, which takes it for granted as a given or, worse yet, treats it as somehow natural, must inevitably reinscribe and may even serve in effect to justify the exclusions. As these queer students see the matter, we historians should no more assume national difference and use it to set agendas for inquiry or to frame narratives than we should assume sexual difference and use it to set agendas for inquiry or to frame narratives. Their question, the question they would prefer to ask, is: how is difference, national difference, or, for that matter, sexual difference, produced, maintained, reproduced? And they'd typically like to see their question about national difference accompany or underwrite virtually any use of the nation-state in any historical narrative. In other words, the nation-state shouldn't, in their view, be a given or a framework but rather a focus of historical inquiry, explanation, and narrative.

So these queer students I've lately taught respect and value the works of lesbian/gay history I assign but don't own them as did their lesbian and gay predecessors in the same classroom. Typically, the queers criticize the trope of marginalization that organizes many of these historical narratives; they resist the representation, relatively usual in these narratives, of persons as distinct, separate, and individual beings with deep subjectivity, who are capable of original and decisive action; they wax indignant whenever they find that these narratives figure persons as achieving authenticity through sex; and they worry about the way most of these narratives are framed by the nation-state. To put their position differently, they are interested in destabilizing identity in virtually every sense, in the past as well as in the present, and they want the performance of that destabilization to be always primary. In the end, they sometimes imply or even say to me—and I have to tell you that I find this reaction of theirs painful—that the lesbian and gay histories I assign are not their history.

My own assessment of the value and cogency of the queer critique of lesbian/gay history produced by these students is mixed. But since my chief purpose here is neither to praise nor to blame these students but rather to try to clarify both their position as history readers and the consequences of that position, I won't expound my assessment. Instead, I'll comment briefly on two aspects of the cultural matrix in which these students and their teacher work. First, you will have probably noticed that there are some affinities between the aesthetic and sensibility of these queer students and the widely influential congeries of contemporary positions that goes by the name postmodernism. Most of my students, queer and nonqueer alike, are drawn to postmodernism, but the queer students are, I think, especially eager to claim it for their own. Second, I am a cultural historian, and yet I teach my lesbian/gay history courses in an English department. In the United States, English is often friendlier to lesbian/gay history than History is. Throughout the country, lesbian/gay study of all kinds is often sponsored by English departments. If my students are eager to work on texts like Cole Porter lyrics or Dorothy Arzner movies, this may be partly because they have taken lots of English courses and have had more experience in working on texts than on any other kind of data.

Until now, I have concentrated on the discontinuity between the outlook of my queer students and the works of lesbian/gay history I assign to them. I have concentrated on the discontinuity because the students do. The discontinuity is what they talk about most. And as I have already indicated, they sometimes even set aside or affect to set aside these works of lesbian/gay history as belonging to others rather than to themselves. Despite such occasional gestures of setting aside, I believe that they do very much need these works of lesbian and gay history, and they certainly seek them out. I also believe that there is, in fact, more similarity than difference, more continuity than discontinuity, between the queer students and these works of history. I said before that the queer students were interested in destabilizing identity in the past as well as in the present, and that they wanted the performance of that destabilization to be always primary. What these works of history do—all I've referred to—is to historicize identity. From historicizing to destabilizing is arguably just a step.

Along with lesbian/gay history books, I sometimes also assign what history teachers call primary sources—documents, memoirs, fictions, poems. There is one poem that the queer students greatly admire. It is Frank O'Hara's 1960 ode of tribute to the French Negro poets of negritude, especially Aimé Césaire. In this ode, O'Hara makes clear that he addresses Césaire and the other francophone exponents of negritude from his own grounding in lesbian/gay culture, life, and struggle in New York City, and in the last line says:

> ... dying in black and white we fight for what we love not are.[14]

When I observe how very eagerly the queer students claim these words, and how intensely they need and also contend with the history they don't feel fully enabled to claim, I believe I know that far more unites than divides lesbian, gay, and queer.

American Studies, Queer Studies

I want to comment on the early years of American Studies as a field of study, a discipline. My object isn't to provide a full account of the development of that discipline or to survey all the various university settings where American Studies was first produced—including, for instance, the University of Washington, Yale University, and the University of Minnesota. Instead, I'm going to focus on just one important site and time, Harvard University, 1929 to 1950; on one leading scholar who taught there then, Francis Otto Matthiessen, a white and well-to-do male homosexual leftist; on Matthiessen's colleagues, students, critics, and opponents, from Harvard and elsewhere; on the work that Matthiessen and these others produced in exchange with one another and in response to one another; and finally, on why and how that work matters or ought to matter now.

Even limiting myself in this way, I am aware that I take on more than I can easily do justice to. Consider for a moment just the students. These students, so many, so influential, included writers like James Agee and Charles Olson and John Ashbery and Richard Wilbur and Robert Coles, historians like Edmund Morgan and Daniel Boorstin and Staughton Lynd and Henry May, literary critics like Leo Marx and Harry Levin and C. L. Barber. I cannot hope to account for all of them or adequately for any one of them. I shall have to refer to them all generally. Matthiessen's close colleagues and peers in the arts and humanities were similarly numerous and influential. They included writers like Muriel Rukeyser and Genevieve Taggard and May Sarton and W. H. Auden and T. S. Eliot and Malcom Cowley and Alfred Kazin. Perry Miller, Matthiessen's fellow faculty member at Harvard, in particular deserves focused attention, and I cannot now provide it for him or any other of these colleagues and peers. Still, I think there may be some use in trying to add what little I can to an understanding of that long-gone Matthiessen milieu and its impact on the making of American Studies.

Francis Otto Matthiessen, Matty to most of his friends, was born in California in 1902 but grew up mostly in LaSalle, Illinois, which he always regarded as his hometown.[1] His family was moderately but securely rich. His paternal grandfather had been a successful entrepreneur, a manufacturer of alarm clocks for a mass market, Big Ben Alarm Clocks; and Matthiessen had a trust fund–based income from the time he was a young adult. This trust fund, administered by a Chicago bank, never failed, so far as I can tell, even during the worst years of the Depression. His family sent Matthiessen east for schooling, choosing a relatively obscure preparatory school that wasn't much favored by old Yankee money. Matthiessen would figure as a new money Midwesterner in the East, and the family perhaps felt that such a preparatory school would be more comfortable for him than anything grander and socially more high-toned. After school, Matthiessen went to Yale, where he excelled in the study of English literature, graduating at the head of the class of 1923. At Yale he was also chosen for membership in the secret society Skull and Bones. Since Skull and Bones continues to exist at Yale and is still secret, I don't know and cannot learn much about its ways and rituals. But judging from the unpublished letters I have read in the Matthiessen papers, letters between Matthiessen and his fellow members of Bones, I believe I can tell this: Every year, a very small number of Yale undergraduates were chosen for the club, presumably by the members already belonging. Members were expected to share confidences with one another, to keep these confidences confidential, and to give one another virtually unconditional acceptance, support, and respect as long as they lived. I think I can also tell that Matthiessen, who had realized in his early teens that he was sexually attracted to other men, revealed his sexual interests to Skull and Bones. Under the seal of absolute confidentiality he told them that he was an invert and a homosexual—these were the terms he typically used of himself—and he described for them his struggle to live his life without acting on his desires—desires that he then saw as degraded and degrading.[2] I should add that with no other people, apart from Bones members and the women whom they eventually married, so far as I can tell, did Matthiessen ever feel he could be similarly forthright about his homosexuality. And so Skull and Bones was, as he saw the matter, the best and safest haven in his life, and he always treasured his membership in Skull and Bones accordingly.

After Yale Matthiessen did graduate work in English literature at Oxford, where he held a Rhodes scholarship, and at Harvard. While crossing the Atlantic on an ocean liner during his time at Oxford, he met another passenger, the painter Russell Cheney, who was twenty years older than Matthiessen. Like Matthiessen, Cheney was an independently wealthy white Yale graduate who considered himself homosexual, and he too was a member of Skull and Bones. There was a strong mutual attraction, and before the end of the voyage they had declared their love to one another and had decided to spend their lives together. For some months Matthiessen held to the view that their love should be without physical expression.[3] Soon, though, Matthiessen overcame or set aside his moral objection to acting erotically on his desires and, relenting in his own favor, agreed to let the relationship be sexual. It continued so probably until Cheney's death, some twenty years later. But they typically represented the relationship to family and associates discreetly as a spiritual friendship. In public settings, too, as for instance in print, Matthiessen described Cheney as a "friend."[4] After

Matthiessen took up a teaching post at Harvard in 1929, he lived mostly in Boston in an apartment on Beacon Hill, while Cheney lived often at a country home they bought at Kittery, in Maine, far from prying eyes.

Matthiessen made a strong impact on students and colleagues at Harvard. At the start of his Harvard appointment, he taught mostly Elizabethan tragedy. Soon, however, he turned to teaching American literature and made it the focus of his research interests as well. When he began to teach American literature, he was one of only two faculty at Harvard who were doing so. He especially liked to lecture on democratic culture: what it was, how it had developed in the United States, how it might be reformed or even transformed, what had been written about it in the nineteenth century and after, and above all how that body of American writing on democratic culture related, or might be related, to the political struggles of the 1930s and 1940s, especially to the struggles against fascism and for socialism. Matthiessen was extraordinarily effective as a teacher. His devotion to teaching, his fine intelligence, and his willingness to teach American literature when relatively few others were willing to do so—these were all probably part of the cause of his effectiveness. But his insistence on seeing the literature he taught as a resource in the politics of his own time was almost certainly part of the cause, too. No other literature professor at Harvard was similarly concerned with contemporary applications. Many of Matthiessen's students from the 1930s have testified to the intellectual excitement that his very engaged and always serious teaching produced in them.[5]

Alongside his relationship with Cheney and teaching, Matthiessen also found time to work actively on a wide range of political projects. Since his undergraduate days he had become steadily more radical in outlook. In 1920 he had supported Warren Harding in the presidential election; by the 1930s Matthiessen was a convinced socialist. He joined the Harvard Teachers Union and served as its president. He also served as its delegate to the Boston Central Labor Council, the Massachusetts Federation of Labor, and the American

F. O. Matthiessen at Harvard, 1940s. From Monthly Review *2, no. 6 (October 1950); copyright 1950* Monthly Review.

Federation of Teachers. A staunch defender of the communist head of the Longshoremen's Union, Harry Bridges, whom the federal government sought to deport, Matthiessen served as national chairman of the Citizens Committee for Harry Bridges, whose members and sponsors also included Aaron Copland, Dashiell Hammett, Lillian Hellman, Paul Robeson, Orson Welles, Clifford Odets, Tess Slesinger, and Richard Wright. He helped found the Samuel Adams School in Boston, an adult-education center for workers' education, and he supported it financially. He also provided essential financial support for the independent Marxist journal *Monthly Review*. He became an advocate for equality for women. He spearheaded the Civil Liberties Union opposition to the banning in Boston of Lillian Smith's novel on "miscegenation," *Strange Fruit*. He served as a delegate to the Progressive Party convention that nominated Henry Wallace for president and seconded the nomination, with a speech, as a spokesman for the Massachusetts delegation.

Matthiessen not only taught, not only threw himself into political activism, not only maintained his semiopen, semisecret relationship with Cheney, he also wrote—on Henry James, on Sarah Orne

Jewett, on his friend T. S. Eliot, and, most famously perhaps, on mid-nineteenth-century American culture. He titled the book on the mid–nineteenth century *American Renaissance*. First published in 1941, it is a study of Thoreau, Whitman, Emerson, Melville, and Hawthorne. From the time of its publication, it has been widely regarded as a founding text of the discipline of American Studies.

To celebrate the publication of *American Renaissance*, Matthiessen's students and his fellow members of the Harvard Teachers Union threw a joint gala dinner party. Among those in attendance were many who would play key roles in the decades following in establishing American Studies programs all over the country. Congratulatory letters flowed in from outside Harvard too—from scholars throughout the country, from trade-union activists, from old friends at Skull and Bones. Why was the book greeted with so much applause, so many congratulations, such institution-building fervor? For many students and colleagues, Matthiessen and his work represented a new direction they were eager to follow. American Studies was the name of the direction. What it meant to them then, I should say, was, first of all, a commitment to put America into the university curriculum, as Matthiessen had; second, a commitment to find in America high and worthy thought and art, as Matthiessen had; third, a commitment to bind the literature of the American past in ways liberating and instructive to the politics and history of the American present, as Matthiessen had; and finally, a commitment to affirm the value of democracy and to endeavor to improve it, as Matthiessen had. American Studies would mean a different range of commitments in later times and in other places, but that was what it meant to students and colleagues in Matthiessen's milieu at the time of the publication of *American Renaissance*. For them Matthiessen was an icon and his book a pillar of fire to guide them on their way.

And yet I believe that most did not wholly and unqualifiedly like the book. I speak generally, of course, and according to my impressions. Reading their tributes, their congratulations, in letters and speeches and reviews, I notice some edginess, some reserve, even some wariness. So far as I can tell, what produces the edginess, reserve, and wariness is a sense of an erotic focus in the book, a focus that is somehow obtrusive though never quite explicit. Did they know that Matthiessen personally was, as he would have put it, homosexual? Cheney was often far away from Harvard, out of sight. But Matthiessen's older colleagues would have met him, might easily have guessed something about the relationship of these two "friends." For some of Matthiessen's graduate students and younger colleagues—and I quote now from a piece by two of them—"Matty's homosexuality was suggested, if at all, only by the fact that his circle was more predominantly heterosexual than was usual in Harvard literary groups of the time" and that he was exceptionally "hostile to homosexual colleagues."[6] So some graduate students and younger colleagues would perhaps have guessed.

Whether or not they knew or guessed something of Matthiessen's own homosexuality, they were surely right to sense an erotic focus in the book. It is hinted at in the dedication to two men, friends of Matthiessen's, who, he says, "have taught me most about the possibilities of life in America." It is hinted at in the book's select cast of characters—Thoreau, Melville, Whitman, Hawthorne, and Emerson—the first three of whom were then, as they are now, particularly amenable to appropriation by gay readers in search of predecessors. It is hinted at in the reproduction, so central to the book, of Thomas Eakins's great painting of naked young men, "The Swimming Hole." It is hinted at in Matthiessen's strange analysis of that painting. He says that the design "matches" the designs "of the Italian Renaissance,"[7] as though to convey what he means by "renaissance," whether in sixteenth-century Italy or nineteenth-century America. It is hinted at in the introduction, which says that the book is concerned chiefly with "the secret" of the "life" of the texts it discusses.[8] Matthiessen's explicit theme is the culture of democracy in mid-nineteenth-century America. What is inexplicit,[9] what is merely suggested, is the question the book frames without asking: what was the erotic meaning of that democracy, the erotic dynamic, the ties, affections, affiliations, that bound together those white men, supposititiously equal, supposititiously brothers, who were the privileged subjects of the old republic? And if we could know that erotic dynamic, would we know something pertinent to the tasks of improving and deepening and expanding and advancing and even reconstructing democracy in the present? Whitman had long before described the old democracy as "boys, together clinging, fulfilling our foray." What was that "clinging"? Was the old democracy distinguishable from white male homosexuality as Matthiessen knew it, and if so, how? Matthiessen would never have put this question explicitly, any more than he would have explicitly represented his own relationship with Cheney to family, students, and colleagues. But the question is framed there in the book nonetheless.

And the question was heard by Matthiessen's readers—students, colleagues, coworkers in the vineyard of American Studies, who were, as I said before, made edgy by the book. W. H. Auden, who had lately immigrated to the United States, heard the question too. A gay man himself, he wasn't made edgy by it; he joked and teased about it instead. In a very campy letter to Matthiessen, Auden wrote, "[apparently] America the Beautiful, True, and Good is a *MONASTERY* surrounded by savage elks and poisonous rotarians."[10] I have found no copy of Matthiessen's reply. Many others outside of Matthiessen's milieu heard as well, for responses to the question the book frames but never asks or even articulates came cascading, and the cascade has continued virtually to the present day. In fact, one way of characterizing at least one strain, maybe one straight masculinist strain, in the development of the literary side of American Studies since Matthiessen's day, would be as a persistent avoidance of Matthiessen's unasked question through the indignant establishment of a series of counterpositions designed to make the question fade away.

I will briefly survey some of these responses. Charles Olson, the poet, studied closely with Matthiessen for three years. While still a student, Olson discovered some important sources on Hawthorne and Melville. Matthiessen drew on these sources, acknowledging Olson's discovery of them, in *American Renaissance*. After Olson dropped out of graduate school, he set himself to writing a prose poem on Melville. He titled it *Call Me Ishmael*. It first appeared in print in 1947, and it is certainly written against *American Renaissance*. In that prose poem, as also in his later writings on Melville, Olson made clear that he despised what he called the "amorous" approach to Melville's fiction and the delight some critics took in Melville's "epicene . . . 'soft, hermaphroditical'" characters. Melville's greatness was nothing to do with democratic fraternity, with clinging, as Whitman had called it, but rather with space. Olson spelled "space" with capital letters. "SPACE," he insisted, is "the central fact to man born in America." Melville, he said, saw this; Melville understood that the Pacific, for Americans, would be a "20th century Great West." It would be the "HEART-SEA," "twin and rival of the HEARTLAND." Olson's counterposition, then, to Matthiessen's unasked question was: democracy was and must be expansion, empire. It was nothing to do with homosexuality. "We must go over space," Olson says, "or we wither."[11]

For another example, take Yvors Winters at Stanford, who invented a character called Professor X and responded to him with contempt in the course of an essay on the poet Hart Crane, an essay that first appeared, like Olson's prose poem, in 1947. The essay was titled "The Significance of 'The Bridge' by Hart Crane, or What Are We to Think of Professor X"? Professor X, Winters said, was a composite portrait of many contemporary American teachers, particularly specialists on American literature or history, but clearly Matthiessen was the chief target. Winters argued that Hart Crane's life and views, which he regarded as fundamentally immoral, derived directly from Emerson and Whitman. Professor X, though a "gentleman and a scholar," as Winters put it, was to be blamed for admiring Emerson and Whitman and for teaching them to the young as admirable. Crane's homosexuality, his alcoholism, his suicide were just the sort of outcome to be expected as Professor X's teaching gained ground. For "if the impulses are indulged . . . passionately," as Winters asserted Emerson and Whitman say they should be, then they could lead only to "madness."[12] Winter's counterposition to

Matthiessen's unasked question was that Emerson and Whitman were advocates of self-indulgence leading to madness. Their writing had therefore everything to do with homosexuality, nothing at all to do with democracy, and their avatars and exponents, such as Matthiessen, were corrupters of the young.

Leslie Fiedler also confronted Matthiessen, in his much-discussed and widely distributed 1960 book, *Love and Death in the American Novel*. It is above all Matthiessen's choice of texts, his canon, that Fiedler assumed; he admitted he accepted that canon, "lock, stock, and barrel," at least at the start.[13] And it is, I should say, Matthiessen's big book that Fiedler aimed to displace with his own. Fiedler famously argued that American fiction hadn't imagined, represented, or dealt with "adult heterosexual love." For Fiedler this was a pathological failing. American literature was problematical and death-driven, as Fiedler viewed it, in the measure that it was, as he said, obsessed with childish "homosexuality."[14] Fiedler's counterposition to Matthiessen's unasked question was: American novels were like children incapable of emotional maturation. Their homosexuality was evident, of course, but had nothing to do with democracy. It was rather a symptom of a malaise, in them and in the society that had produced them, a malaise that a right-thinking critic, like Fiedler himself, would endeavor to cure or treat or at least to expose.

Stanley Cavell is one last example, from the recent past and the present. He wrote extensively on Thoreau and Emerson in the 1980s and early 1990s and is still writing on Emerson. Especially crucial to this corpus of writing is his 1990 book *Conditions Handsome and Unhandsome: The Constitution of Emersonian Perfectionism*, in which he continued the project so long identified with Matthiessen of interpreting Emerson as a thoughtful exponent of democracy. Just as democracy was the great achievement of modernity, Cavell argued, so Emerson was the great philosopher of modernity. At the heart of Emerson's work, Cavell found a democratic theory of moral conduct, and Cavell maintained that this theory of moral conduct should be understood as modeled on and representable by the right and meet conversation of husband and wife in a mature marriage. Cavell also discovered intimations of a similar or related theory in the practice of conversation in the Platonic dialogues, among interlocutors who were men. Cavell occasionally wrote too in ways that suggested that what he regarded as fundamental conversation might be conducted with any "friend." But for Cavell, and for his great reading of democratic philosophy, the model—the touchstone—was certainly heterosexual marriage.[15] His counter-position to Matthiessen's unasked question was: Emerson's writing had everything to do with democracy, apparently little or nothing to do with homosexuality. What Emerson showed was that mature, heterosexual marriage was somehow the very form of democratic morality and culture.

These various assertions of counterpositions to Matthiessen's un-asked question—Olson's, Winter's, Fiedler's, Cavell's—have taken us far beyond Matthiessen's milieu at Harvard. I want to turn back to that milieu and comment on the end of Matthiessen's life and career. I left off at the gala dinner that Matthiessen's students and colleagues threw in 1941 to celebrate the publication of *American Renaissance*. That dinner was perhaps the high point of Matthiessen's popularity and success and happiness at Harvard.[16] Afterward came loss. For one thing, the reception of the book once the gala party was done never really met his expectations. I think that it is also possible that he felt some measure of regret and humiliation about what he hadn't quite articulated in the book, about the question he had never really asked. Then, too, during the war his graduate students were mostly away on military duty, and Harvard was transformed into a technical school. Matthiessen felt out of place. In 1945 Cheney died, a devastating blow, leaving Matthiessen bereft and alone. Nor could he secure support in his mourning in his milieu at Harvard or in the world of American Studies beyond Harvard, for who could give it? His relationship with Cheney had always, perhaps nec-essarily, been undiscussable with colleagues and students. Of course, letters of condolence flowed in, but they only heightened his sadness because they acknowledged nothing of the actuality of the relationship. Here is an excerpt from a letter from the distinguished novelist and poet Robert Penn Warren; it may be taken as typical of the others: "I envy you your acquaintance with Cheney. He must have been extraordinarily rewarding company."[17]

More troubles followed. As the intensified anticommunism and homophobia of the Cold War era took hold at Harvard and throughout the country during the late 1940s, Matthiessen, who insisted on avowing his own socialism and on defending communists whenever they were at risk, suddenly found himself a pariah. Longtime faculty colleagues avoided him. *Life* magazine published his name in a list of fifty prominent dupes of the communist conspiracy. Columnists in the local press, especially the *Boston Herald,* wrote attack after attack on him. Anticommunist investigators from the government wanted him to answer questions. Harvard's senior administration, which had never much liked him, started to harass him openly. Irving Howe declared in the journal *Partisan Review,* in the course of a review of one of Matthiessen's books: "if some of us" in the United States "ever end our days in a communist corrective labor camp it might well be because of . . . intellectuals like F. O. Matthiessen."[18] I should add that Matthiessen kept in his papers virtually no reviews or notices of his books, but he kept this hateful review by Howe.

Worst of all from Matthiessen's perspective, students turned away from him. Formerly a hero to students, he was now to many of them a communist fellow traveler and therefore a wrongdoer. Probably the most hurtful rebuff from students was the 1949 decision of the student liberal group, the Liberal Union, to require that Matthiessen step down as faculty sponsor. I have found a draft of Matthiessen's reply to the liberal students' letter notifying him of his dismissal in which he says: "In the light of your letter, I am very glad not to be any longer an adviser or sponsor of the Harvard Liberal Union, but I would have expected your notice of services-no-longer required would have contained the minimum expression of gratitude normal in such circumstances. You obviously do not understand the grounds on which I originally agreed to be a sponsor. My politics have never coincided with those of your organization. . . . The primary role of a sponsor, as I have understood it, amounts to standing up and saying to the conservative administration that a student liberal organization has a right to exist. I still take that view with regard to the Liberal Union, even though you have apparently now grown so respectable as to find it prudential to sever your tenuous connection with a radical professor."[19] That is the heart of the draft reply. A little more than a year after he wrote that draft, on April 1, 1950, he killed himself. He rented a room in a hotel in downtown Boston and jumped out the window. On the dresser in the hotel room he left a short note, saying, ". . . I can no longer believe that I can continue to be of use to my profession and my friends."[20] He also left his Skull and Bones ring, which he had carefully removed so that it would not be damaged in his fall.

I return now to Matthiessen's *American Renaissance* and to the account I offered of the way in which a certain strain of American Studies scholarship has endeavored to avoid the question that book frames but doesn't ask. I suggested that this strain of American Studies avoided the unasked question by fronting it with one counterposition after another. I also suggested that an important purpose of these counterpositions was to make Matthiessen's unasked question fade away. These counterpositions, in other words, prevent, obviate the question. And I further suggested that the content of the question was: what was the erotic meaning of nineteenth-century American democracy? What was the erotic dynamic, the ties, affections, affiliations, that bound together the white men who were the privileged subjects of the old republic?

I conclude with two metaphors.

I understand that the term "asymptote" is used in mathematics to name "the line that is the limiting position which the tangent to a curve approaches, as the point of contact recedes indefinitely along an infinite branch of the curve."[21] In this sense, I could say that Matthiessen's unasked question has for a long time now been the asymptote to American Studies. Or perhaps a metaphor drawn from psychoanalysis rather than mathematics would be preferable.

American Studies as a discipline, I could say, is a well-received and much-validated set of reaction formations to questions like Matthiessen's, questions framed at the start of the discipline's development but immediately and thoroughly deflected, sacrificed, and repressed, as were the questioners themselves. In this second, psychoanalytic metaphor, Queer Studies would figure as present at the start of American Studies, as always part of the unconscious of American Studies. And the future of American Studies would then depend in large measure on whether or not that unconscious is permitted to return.

New York City
Gay Liberation and
the Queer Commuters

We aren't easily intimidated.
And yet we are always frightened . . .
JOHN ASHBERY, GIRLS ON THE RUN

New York City's Gay Liberation Front, or GLF, as it was often called in its heyday, was founded during the summer of 1969 shortly after the Stonewall riot—a riot sparked by a police raid of a gay bar in Greenwich Village. Much good historical work has been done since the founding of GLF, especially during the 1980s and 1990s, on the antecedents and the goals of the organization and of the movement it helped to make. We now have detailed accounts, for instance, of the homophile clubs such as Mattachine and the Daughters of Bilitis that chronologically preceded GLF and influenced it even as GLF quarreled with their policies and practices—policies and practices that the GLFers regarded as timid and accommodationist. We now have a range of studies of sixties social formations like second-wave feminism, the civil rights movement, the black power movement, and the antiwar movement; and all of these social formations made an important impact on GLF, on its tactics, its commitments, and its mode of expression. We now have a book on the Stonewall riot that provides an hour-by-hour narrative of the resistance of the queer bar patrons and passersby to the police raid. And some surely would argue that New York City's GLF was precipitated from the experience of that riot. Finally, there is now much useful and closely researched historical work on networks and communities in the period before 1969—networks and communities of lesbians and bulldaggers and fairies and transgenderists and bisexuals and femmes and gays and butches, in New York City and Cherry Grove and Philadelphia and Buffalo and Boston and San Francisco and elsewhere. This knowledge of networks and communities has undoubtedly enhanced our understanding of the social matrix in which GLF emerged.[1]

Yet I believe that our historical grasp on GLF and its antecedents is nevertheless still weak. I would like to comment, if only schematically, on one underexplored aspect of the antecedents and character of New York City's GLF. I want to draw attention to a set of anglophone writers—writers of fiction and poetry mostly but also of essays and diaries—who published queer-themed work during the two decades preceding 1969. This work, it seems to me, was enormously productive for GLF, its members, and its milieu, and significantly contributed to the development of its outlook and values. The writers to whom I refer are James Baldwin, Elizabeth Bishop, Jane Bowles, Paul Bowles, William Burroughs, Allen Ginsberg, Paul Goodman, Frank O'Hara, and Ned Rorem. Of these writers only Ginsberg has, so far as I know, been linked even peripherally in any historical argument to gay liberation.[2] But all of them mattered centrally to gay liberation, and if we attend to them and their work, there is, I think, this potential gain: we may see something at least of the sources of the GLF way of talking about the erotic in an anticolonialist frame of reference.

Before I say more about these writers and their work, I want to speculate on the reasons that they and their work are relatively neglected in the histories we now have of GLF and of the movement it helped to create, for this relative neglect would seem to require explanation. After all, these writers were all literary and intellectual forces present to anglophone readers in the 1960s. Some of their work was very widely distributed and extensively reviewed. Even those like Rorem, who had comparatively small audiences, were arguably as much read as were homophile journals such as the *Ladder* and the *Mattachine Review*. All of these writers provided representations of queer life for audiences starved for just such representations. Some, such as Ginsberg, Goodman, and O'Hara, were also beloved, charismatic figures, much involved in parts of New York City's queer social and cultural scene. And lots, maybe most, of the GLFers, their friends, and their hangers-on were college students, readers as a matter of course. If I am right to say that there has been a relative neglect of these writers in our histories, I'd suggest that the cause is this: the mode of social history that came of age in America in the 1970s, and grew to maturity and achieved many fine successes in the era following, has made little room for writing as a productive force.

Returning now to the set of writers I listed before, I should perhaps make clear that I don't see these writers as a school like, say, the Agrarians or the Surrealists. These writers were very different from one another. They did not, as a whole, share an agenda or a style or an allegiance to a particular literary predecessor or contemporary. Nor did each of them admire all the others. Quite to the contrary: Bishop thought that Ginsberg's poetry was hopelessly passé; Rorem thought that Burroughs was dreadful; O'Hara thought that Baldwin's essays and fiction were bombastic.[3] Similarly, I don't say that this set of writers constituted a generation. Paul Bowles was considerably older than Rorem, Burroughs older than Ginsberg. Nor do I mean to suggest that these writers shared a single political outlook, for they did not. Bishop was an anticommunist liberal; Jane Bowles and Paul Bowles were communists between 1938 and 1940 and never, in my opinion, wholly transcended or abandoned this early commitment; Burroughs was perhaps fundamentally an anarchist. Shortly before Ginsberg died, he said of Burroughs, I think rightly, that one could read his loathing for the state even in his cut-up writings, which were randomly joined bits and pieces.[4] O'Hara's first and formative political commitment was to the anti-sacerdotalist and populist ideals of the Spanish Republic, though the Republic had perished before he was grown, and for him this commitment probably remained the chief standard by which he judged political issues and problems throughout his life. These descriptions of political positions, as I have just given them, are of course too summary, scanty, and unnuanced to be of much use. Their only purpose here is to indicate a considerable range of difference among these writers.

If these writers weren't united by shared literary purposes as a school, or by mutual regard, or by age as a generation, or by a shared political outlook, what do I see that makes them a set? Why do I join them together in this history? First, all left or were driven out of the United States during the post–World War II era, and most stayed away for long stretches of time—Baldwin in France and Turkey; Bishop in Brazil; Paul Bowles in Tangier and Ceylon; Jane Bowles in Tangier; Burroughs in Central America and Tangier; Ginsberg in India, Tangier, Czechoslovakia, and France; Goodman in Italy; Rorem in France and Morocco. O'Hara was away from the United States less than the others, but he too traveled—in France, Spain, the Netherlands, and Yugoslavia. Second, all of them were personally and artistically interested in same-sex eroticism, and all made the representation of such eroticism a part of their writing. Third, all were convinced that decolonization was a paramount aspect of the world as they observed and knew it while they lived and traveled outside the United States, and most wrote in ways that inflected that conviction. Burroughs and Paul Bowles represented Moslem nationalism in their fictions; Ginsberg represented anti-Soviet insurgency in Eastern Europe in his poetry; Bishop represented Brazilian poverty and banditry in her poetry; Rorem represented the last and beleaguered era of the French colonial civil service in North Africa in his diaries. In attitude these writers tended to be anticolonialist, though only ambivalently so, and their writings often, of course, reproduced conventional colonialist tropes and values. Moreover, when they lived outside the United States they surely made use of their position of privilege as Americans to garner personal advantages.[5]

I said that all these writers left, or were driven out of, the United

States during the post–World War II era, and I should explain why they left, why they were driven out. As America's politics and society were chilled by the Cold War, starting roughly in the late 1940s, old fears and hatreds of queers, quite as much as of communists, grew to be stronger and more widely distributed than they had been before and were also given weight in new statutes and government policies, as well as in stern enforcement of long-standing statutes and government policies. So, for instance, male-male sexual acts were illegal, felonies, in every state in the union throughout the forties and the fifties, and arrests and prosecutions were by no means uncommon. Female-female sexual acts were very rarely illegal, but the police could and did during this period raid lesbian social venues, prosecuting those caught on a variety of charges ranging from disorderly conduct to lascivious carriage. For those known or thought to be queer, there was also a very real and present risk of job loss. Large-scale firings from federal government employment began in the late 1940s, but the pace of firings quickened sharply in 1953 when President Dwight Eisenhower issued his Executive Order 10450, declaring that sexual perverts were presumptively unfit for any federal government job whatsoever. Another executive order was later issued, extending the ban on the employment of perverts to all those businesses that held contracts from the Department of Defense. Such contracts were held by many, maybe even most, of America's major industrial corporations. Private employers, even those that didn't hold Department of Defense contracts, also often fired queers, sometimes because they were informally pressured to do so by local police forces or the FBI. State and local governments largely followed the example of the federal government in firing queers—in their civil service, in their public schools, in their hospitals, and in their libraries. In addition, state governments sometimes revoked the professional licenses of those known to be queer. During the 1950s, California revoked licenses for queers who practiced as doctors, dentists, lawyers, pharmacists, or morticians.[6] From about 1950 until about 1961, even those colleges and universities that were willing to hire queers were almost always disposed to fire any of them, including any tenured faculty member, who was arrested on a sex charge, and such arrests were made.[7]

For the writers I have listed, and for queers generally, nothing like a reasonably secure life in sex or work was at all possible in the United States from the late forties until the early sixties. All of these writers wanted a life that included sex, and since none of them

Elizabeth Bishop, 1940s. Courtesy of Special Collections, Vassar College Libraries. Photograph by Joseph Breitenbach.

could earn enough on which to live from writing alone, all of them wanted jobs as well as sex. On both these fronts they were blocked or threatened. Let me give an example of the blockage and threat at a particular site, one important cultural institution and employer, the Library of Congress, which at various times actually employed two of these writers, Bishop and Paul Bowles. Between 1947 and 1956, the managers of the Library of Congress arranged for the investigation of more than 2,200 of its employees to determine whether or not they were subversives or sexual perverts. Most of those investigated were cleared, to use the language of the day. But six were fired or forced to resign on suspicion of leftism. Ten were fired as sexual perverts. No record exists of the number who were refused as new hires on either or both of these same two grounds.[8] Bishop could work at the Library as poetry consultant in 1949, earning $5,000,[9] a big sum then, only because she concealed her lesbianism assiduously. In fact, she concealed it as long as she remained in the United States. Of course, the practice of conceal-ment and the ongoing risk of exposure and disgrace put her under great stress and almost certainly contributed to the depression from which she suffered acutely and painfully during her time at the Library. She left the United States for Brazil in 1951 and stayed there, with just occasional trips back, for most of the next twenty years. Paul Bowles left the United States for Tangier in 1947, as the Cold War started up. He was well known to be both a former com-munist and a queer. Despite his distinction as a writer and com-poser, the Library managers could hardly have offered him a post during this period to work at the Library in Washington, D.C. That would have been unthinkable. But the managers could hire him in 1959, with money provided by the Ford Foundation, to record the indigenous music of Morocco for their music collection. Bowles was glad for the job; he needed the money badly. And the manag-ers were presumably satisfied that so long as he worked for them in Morocco and on a Ford Foundation grant, there could be no loss of good standing for the Library. Bowles remained abroad, with only occasional trips back, until he died in Tangier, his home for more than fifty years, in November 1999.[10]

Bad as the prospect for queers was at the Library of Congress, it was in no way atypical. On the contrary, it was typical of the prospect for queers in professional employment generally throughout the United States during this period. Some queer writers, it is true, succeeded in keeping professional jobs throughout these difficult years, either because of luck or because of their success in hiding their sexual interests or because of their skill in steering past the shoals of hate and fear rising on all sides. Robin Blaser, for example, held onto a good position at the Widener Library at Harvard. Some others managed to find a job at one of the very few cultural institutions that remained relatively queer-friendly, such as the Museum of Modern Art, where O'Hara worked, along with several other distinguished queer writers who on occasion sheltered there, including James Schuyler. But professional opportunities were rare and chancy. For queer writers in the United States, one common way to cope was to try to obtain menial employment. Burroughs worked as a pest exterminator, Ginsberg as a baggage handler for Greyhound Bus Lines, Robert Duncan as a typist. Such jobs as these were likely to fall below the level of political surveillance.

These blockages and threats that I have described, blockages and threats to the making of a life secure for sex and work, were in some measure present to all queer writers and to queers generally, but were especially problematic for those queers at the bottom of America's hierarchies of race, class, and gender. For them, there was of course more vulnerability. Of the writers I have listed, all were white except Baldwin, who was black. Baldwin said that during this period he felt that if he remained in America he would eventually "go under." He left the country in 1948, with just $40 to his name.[11] But virtually all queers felt at risk or uneasy, even those in the upper reaches of the hierarchies. Consider the case of the poet James Merrill—a white gay man, rich from the time he was five years old, when his father (the head of Merrill Lynch, then as now the biggest retail stock brokerage firm in the world) had conferred on him an irrevocable trust fund worth a fortune. Merrill believed that he was safe, but even he was affected by panic—the panic of another. His mother, fearing that publicity might render him "unemployable" and a "security risk," and acting without his permission—in order, as she thought, to protect him—destroyed, to his great distress, all the letters he had ever received from the gay men with whom he had intimately corresponded. Merrill left the country in 1950, the same year his mother destroyed his letters, meaning to stay away as long as he could.[12] Or consider the case of Paul Bowles. He left the country, as I mentioned before, in 1947, returning now and then for visits, some lasting as long as ten months. During none of these visits back to the United States, as he told his biographer Millicent Dillon, did he ever have sex. She asked him why he did not. He replied, explaining his sense of the risk, "because of the disapproval of society, . . . the presence of the police, the possibility of blackmail."[13]

For each of the writers who left the country, the mix of motives was of course different. No life is strictly comparable to any other.

James Baldwin, 1965. Photograph by Rick Stafford; copyright Rick Stafford.

But for all, the wish to find more favorable sites for work and sex was a part of the mix. I am going to call the writers I have listed, who left or were driven out of the United States during the Cold War and who later came to influence the GLF, the Queer Commuters. I say "queer" because most of them used that term self-referentially, and moreover, it was especially important to three of them—Burroughs, Goodman, and Ginsberg (Ginsberg famously wrote in his 1956 poem "America," ". . . I am putting my queer shoulder to the wheel").[14] As for the term "commuter," I take that from Baldwin, who apparently preferred it as a self-description to the terms "exile" and "expatriate."[15] He seems to have thought that "commuter" was more nearly accurate than either of those other terms. For like all these others, he did not stay away from the United States continuously, but traveled back and forth. I believe that Baldwin preferred the term "commuter" for another reason as well: "commuter" was an ironic allusion to the fifties mainstream in America. Although I follow Baldwin in using and preferring the term "commuter," I should perhaps also say that there was a sense in which all of these writers might feel like exiles, both when they were in the United States and when they were away. Goodman, who, as a queer, was fired from three different teaching jobs in succession, captured this sense of exile particularly well in his memoir of his life in the fifties. He subtitled the memoir "Thoughts in a Useless Time," and there he quoted, with an irony much like Baldwin's, from Scripture, in Hebrew as well as English: "because of our sins we are exiled from our land."[16]

How exactly did the writings of the Queer Commuters impact on New York City's GLF—an organization including lots of college students? GLFers, or Liberationists, as they also called themselves, read the Queer Commuters avidly. What did the Liberationists find as they read? I have already noted that all of the Queer Commuters represented same-sex eroticism in their writings, that all came to be convinced as they traveled away from the United States that decolonization was a paramount aspect of the post–World War II globe, and that most wrote in ways that inflected their conviction of the paramountcy of decolonization. Living where they did, they could hardly escape notice of the paramountcy of decolonization. Faulkner, Bellow, Flannery O'Connor, Welty, Lowell, Mailer, Malamud might know little of it, living and writing within the United States. But as Paul Bowles, based in Tangier, said in 1954, "there was no alternative to recording the process of violent transformation."[17] So, Bowles's 1955 novel *The Spider's House* and Burroughs's 1959 novel *Naked Lunch* are the first widely circulated and perhaps still the most remarkable representations of resurgent Islam in anglophone American literature. What the Liberationists learned or rather appropriated from these writers, and perhaps from others whom I haven't yet tracked, was a repertory of means for figuring the queer erotic and its claims in a framework in which decolonization mattered most.

Now, let me make a careful distinction if I can. I don't want to say that the Liberationists learned to be anticolonialist from the Queer Commuters. First of all, the Queer Commuters weren't anticolonialist consistently. Second, everything in the immediate political experience of these mostly very young Liberationists tended to teach them the lesson of anticolonialism. Like virtually all other American radicals of the late sixties and early seventies, the Liberationists were intensely opposed to the American war against Vietnam, a war that they saw as a colonialist war. The Liberationists were anticolonialist from the start. What they took from their elders, the Queer Commuters, wasn't a quarrel with colonialism. The Liberationists already had that quarrel in hand. What they took from the Queer Commuters was rather a rhetoric for connecting queerness to decolonization and its struggles.

I want to offer three brief examples of what the Liberationists found in the writings of the Queer Commuters and of how, it seems to me, the Liberationists read and understood what they found there. Take Baldwin's 1955 novel, *Giovanni's Room*, published originally in England, since at first Baldwin's American publisher wouldn't accept it—a story of David, a well-to-do white American living in Paris. David betrays a woman whom he pretends to love. He loves and makes love with a man, Giovanni, but then betrays him, too, and virtually causes his death. Both of David's betrayals are figured as motivated by fear—fear of homosexual desire, perhaps also of self-knowledge, perhaps even of love as such. In the novel's first paragraph, David, as narrator, describes himself while he observes his reflection in the "darkening" glass of the windowpane. "My reflection is tall," he writes, "perhaps rather like an arrow, my blond hair gleams. My face is a face you have seen many times. My ancestors conquered a continent, pushing across death-laden plains." Here the scriptural reference, to seeing through a glass darkly, is of course unmistakable. So, too, is the imagery that ties David, the failed lover and betrayer, to a long history of white colonialist conquest and death dealing across the American continent. At the end of the novel, the dark glass recurs. It is nighttime, though nearly morning, and David stands before "a large mirror" where he looks on his "troubling sex" and wonders "how it can be redeemed." When morning comes, he feels "the dreadful weight of hope."

For Liberationist readers, *Giovanni's Room* could serve as a kind of revelation. It taught in familiar scriptural language the familiar scriptural lesson that love was the only alternative to death and destruction. But here the inspiring love denied and betrayed was provocatively perverse. In the novel's dark glass, the GLFers saw their own reflections, searched for the means to comprehend the ties imaged at the start of the book between colonialist conquest and the denial and betrayal of love, and searched too for intimations of what they might yet need to learn to "redeem sex" and, as they often put it, to decolonize America.[18]

Take Elizabeth Bishop as another example. By 1965, when she published *Questions of Travel*, Bishop was already well known, at least among lesbian and gay readers, as a lyricist of lesbianism. Her earlier poems, such as "Insomnia," "Invitation to Miss Marianne Moore," and "The Shampoo," had long been understood as yielding

confessional or quasi-confessional representations of lesbian desire.[19] In the context of that understanding, *Questions of Travel* made
its queer impact. Its themes seemed to be both continuous with
Bishop's earlier lesbian-interest poetry yet also startlingly political
in new ways. Much of the book, the whole first part, concerned
Brazil, where Bishop had lived since 1951, and that part was simply
called "Brazil." It consisted of a series of ten poems, the first, "Arrival
at Santos"; the last, "The Burglar of Babylon." From first to last they
provided, or were thought to provide, a dreamy poetic recapitula-
tion of colonialism in Brazil from the point of view of a displaced
and homeless but definitely privileged lesbian traveler who might
be herself a sort of colonizer.

In "Arrival at Santos," the traveler's ship docks in Brazil. When
the traveler disembarks, she is accompanied by a retired policewoman from upstate New York, a Miss Breen, who is about seventy
years old and "six feet tall," an obvious figure of a butch, whose skirt
is snared by the "boat hook" as she climbs down the ship's ladder,
in an almost burlesque comeuppance for the closety skirt. Still
accompanied by this old butch policewoman, her altogether appropriate Virgil, the traveler drives, she says, toward "the interior."
In the next poem the scene shifts to the past, to the beginnings of
Portuguese colonialism in Brazil; the date is "January 1, 1502," and
"the Christians" are disembarking, hoping for "wealth" and "each
out to catch an Indian" woman. That the traveler identifies with
the colonizers, at least in some measure—that she understands the
troubling continuity between her travel enterprise and theirs—is
suggested by her calling them Christians rather than Portuguese,
by her representing them at the moment of disembarkation, and
above all by her figuring each of them as wanting to catch an Indian
woman. This identification, or partial identification, between the
traveler and the colonizers is made plainer still in the next poem,
where the scene shifts to the traveler in the present as she observes
the Brazilian "strangers" around her and asks questions that apply
equally to herself and to the colonizers of long ago, as she and they
together become "we":

Is it right to be watching strangers in a play
in this strangest of theaters?
What childishness is it that while there's a breath of life
in our bodies, we are determined to rush
to see the sun the other way around?

The rest of the poems in the Brazil series develop a perspective on colonialism and neocolonialism in a variety of aspects and consequences and point as well to sources of actual and potential Brazilian resistance, for instance, in the Brazilians' memory of "rights," in their confidence in a "later era" that "will differ," in the pride and vivacity of a poor "black boy" who thinks of himself as a "highlight" of the world. At the end of the series is "The Burglar of Babylon." In this poem, rendered in ballad-like measure, there is an encounter with the army as well as the police, this time deadly. A Brazilian burglar, Micuçú, escapes from jail, wounding two policemen. Desperate, he takes refuge in a Rio slum, "the hill of Babylon," where he grew up and where his auntie still lives, with a million other slum dwellers nearby: "The poor who come to Rio / And can't go home again." The soldiers are deployed there; they find him and kill him.

The traveler is not figured as present in this last of the Brazil poems. But there is a suggestion of something shared between her and Micuçú nonetheless. She has already been represented in the earlier poems of the series as, like him, having no sure home. She too has "come to Rio / And can't go home again." If there is something shared between her and him, however, there is never a gesture of identification. No presumptuous "we" joins her and Micuçú and the other poor in the slums of Rio, as there is a candid "we" that joins her and the colonizers of long ago. And the difference between her homelessness on the one hand, and Micuçú's and the slum dwellers' on the other, is sharply pointed by the contrasting representations of the police who at the start accompany, and the police, then the soldiers, who at the end of the series shoot and kill.[20]

All the poems in the Brazil series were widely read, perhaps especially "The Burglar of Babylon," which appeared in the *New*

Yorker and was so popular that the rock star Donovan thought of turning it into a song.²¹ For readers who saw the United States, like Brazil, as incompletely decolonized and scarred by crowded urban slums where poverty and desperation sometimes bred criminality, the poem was chillingly resonant. Among the GLFers, the poem was perhaps more than resonant. Like the traveler figured in the Brazil series, GLFers might feel that they shared something very palpable with Micuçú and his neighbors on the hill of Babylon. During the Cold War and before—and after—American lesbians and gay men were objects of attack by the state and its criminal laws. Some few such as the Queer Commuters left the United States; the overwhelming majority remained. But even those many who remained were often driven to internal migration. They tended to cluster in big cities, where they could try to build lives together, and, like the traveler figured in the Brazil series and the burglar Micuçú himself, they couldn't "go home again." One of the most remarkable aspects of the Gay Liberation Front was its immense, almost unbounded sympathy with prisoners of the American state, no matter what their crime or supposed crime. A common feature of virtually all of the GLF newspapers and journals that sprang up in 1969 and immediately thereafter was a passionate emphasis on outreach to prisoners and convicts.²² No doubt there was more than one cause for that passionate emphasis on outreach. But I see Micuçú as one among the causes. Or rather, I see the reading of the ballad of Micuçú, in poetic relation to queer lives, as producing a channel through which GLF fellow feeling and effort could flow readily toward prisoners of all colonizing states, including, as the GLFers believed, the American state, which they often called "Babylon."²³

For a final example, take Frank O'Hara's poem "Ode: Salute to the French Negro Poets." This poem, written in 1958, first published in 1960, addressed to Aimé Césaire, and dedicated to the anticolonialist struggle in the French West Indies and in francophone Africa, was a favorite in queer New York. O'Hara begins, as so many other queer poets have done before him and as so many others have done after him, by invoking Whitman. O'Hara stands, he says, as Whitman did "near the sea" and calls "to the spirits of other lands."

But in a marked reversal of what was, and is, often thought of as Whitman's complicity with or support for American expansionism, O'Hara says to those "spirits," "do not spare your wrath upon our shores. . . ." And he goes on to describe his land as part of "the terrible western world." In that world, and in "our fabled times"—presumably *Time* magazine's "the American Century"—

> . . . cowards are shibboleths and one specific love's
> traduced

For contemporary lesbian and gay readers, whose love was certainly traduced during the persecutions of the Cold War era, the long list of prominent, powerful, and undeservedly well-reputed American cowards might saliently include Dwight Eisenhower, the president, and J. Edgar Hoover, the head of the national police. These men's names were shibboleths, and these men were among the loudest and most damaging of the traducers.

In the passage that follows, O'Hara provides a critique of what he elsewhere in the poem calls "closets"—a critique that came to be crucial to the GLF outlook. O'Hara points to the costs of the closet and of reticence more generally, for the poet and for poetry and for the capacity of all people to resist their traducers and despoilers:

> . . . reticence is paid for by a poet in his blood or ceas-
> ing to be
> blood! blood that we have mountains in our veins to
> stand off jackals

In a certain sense, these lines of O'Hara foretold or maybe even constituted the Gay Liberation Front. For if there was one position that ultimately united everyone in GLF, it was a vehement rejection of the closet and of reticence, with a concomitant demand for resistance. But perhaps the most striking aspect of the poem is its address to Aimé Césaire. Through that address the poem tries to communicate to black anticolonialist comrades elsewhere, in the West Indies and in Africa, a lyric summation of the persecution of queers in Cold War America. This lyric summation is conveyed especially by the phrase that comes at the poem's midpoint:

> . . . the pillaging of our desires and allegiances.

For the Liberationists, the poem was a moving contribution to the making of what they hoped would be a transnational consciousness of the various wrongs of colonial and neocolonial state power.[24]

These three brief examples may perhaps suggest something of the ways in which the Liberationists read the Queer Commuters. But I do not mean to imply that the Queer Commuters would necessarily have approved of GLF. Only two of them, Ginsberg and Burroughs, are known to have approved fundamentally.[25] Goodman and Rorem seem to have approved partly, maybe largely;[26] Paul Bowles disapproved intensely;[27] Bishop probably disapproved too;[28] O'Hara died in 1966, before GLF was founded; Jane Bowles was extremely ill during the late sixties and early seventies, too ill to express an opinion; and Baldwin was ambivalent.[29] Those who disapproved or were ambivalent thought of the GLFers as jejune. Those who approved thought of the GLFers as brave and forward-looking. None of the Queer Commuters was a participant in GLF during the years from 1969 to 1974 when the group was active as an organization or as a coherent political tendency.

So that you can also hear how the New York City GLF sounded when it spoke in its own voice, I will quote a short and, I think, characteristic passage on politics from the New York City GLF newspaper, which was called *Come Out*. This passage on politics is couched as a request for journalistic contributions from readers:

> We shall welcome your contribution to *COME OUT* because you understand that the American Code of Sexual Conduct is a large and necessary part of the apparatus which perverts the creative powers of the majority into wars and toils to increase the powers of a deceased minority who wish either to rule over many others or to wallow in the wealth they steal from the lands and people who produced it.[30]

Christopher Street parade, June 25, 1978. Photograph by Bettye-Lane; copyright Bettye-Lane.

In this statement gay liberation was figured as part of a worldwide move away from colonization, toward decolonization. This was just what the GLFers thought that gay liberation was—and I would suggest that, as readers, they came to know how to say so.

So the Queer Commuters, as read and appropriated by the Liberationists, were crucial to the making of GLF and to the long-lasting movement that GLF helped to create. All of the Commuters, I think, were crucial, but none more so than O'Hara. I believe I can best convey a sense of O'Hara's influence by describing a sculpture by the artist Jasper Johns. It is called "Frank O'Hara, Memory Piece." Johns began the sculpture in 1961, at his studio in Edisto, South Carolina, by taking a plaster cast of O'Hara's left foot; he finished the sculpture in 1970, four years after O'Hara's death and at the height of liberationism. The cast of the foot is attached to the top cover of a wooden box filled with sand. Every time the top cover of the box is closed, a fresh O'Hara left footprint appears in the sand, leading the way.[31]

I end with three suggestions.

1. The well-established social-historical practice of always focusing up close on an object of study, such as gay New York, or the Stonewall riot, or New York City queer activism, so as to render a meticulously detailed account of it, is less a matter of method than of superstition. Sometimes the best way to apprehend an object may be to look away from it, to the sources that shape or produce it, even if they are distant—as distant as Tangier or Rio is from the Hudson.

2. Without some attention to the troubles of queer Americans during the Cold War, no analysis of the literature of the period, of its makers, their material position, their politics, and their topics could possibly be satisfactory.

3. The common view of early gay liberation as an identity politics is mistaken. New York City's GLF was not predicated on a commitment to a supposititiously stable or definite identity. It was rather predicated on a commitment to a worldwide struggle for decolonization and its potential human benefits.

Notes

Freud, Male Homosexuality, and the Americans

1. "A Letter from Freud," *American Journal of Psychiatry* 107 (April 1951): 786.

2. Ernest Jones, *The Life and Work of Sigmund Freud*, 3 vols. (New York: Basic Books, 1953–57), 3: 195.

3. Quoted by Herb Spiers and Michael Lynch, "The Gay Rights Freud," *Body Politic* 33 (May 1977): 9; emphasis in original.

4. Ibid.

5. Ibid. This set of letters is part of a group known as the "Rundbriefe," preserved in the Otto Rank Collection and deposited at the Columbia University Library. I quote from translations prepared, and kindly made available to me, by Professor James Steakley (Rank Collection IIa/238, IIa/243, and IIa/248). Probably the most crucial unpublished source for the history of psychoanalytic thought, the "Rundbriefe" are still very little known. But see Patrick Mahony, *Freud as a Writer* (New York: International Universities Press, 1982), 97–98; M. Grotjahn, "Notes on Reading the 'Rundbriefe,'" *Journal of the Otto Rank Association* 9 (1973–74): 35–38; and E. Salomon, "Reactions to Reading the 'Rundbriefe,'" *Journal of the Otto Rank Association* 8 (1973–74): 89–91.

6. See, for instance, Freud's letter of April 13, 1919, to Oscar Pfister, in *The Letters of Sigmund Freud and Oscar Pfister*, ed. H. Meng and E. Freud (New York: Basic Books, 1963), 68.

7. An excerpt from Goetz's memoir in English translation is printed in *Freud As We Knew Him*, ed. H. Ruitenbeek (Detroit: Wayne State University Press, 1973), 266–68. For the full text in the original German, see Bruno Goetz, "Erinnerungen an Sigmund Freud," *Neue Schweizer Rundschau* 20 (May 1952): 3–11. This translation, slightly modified by me, is Dr. Ruitenbeek's.

8. See Jürgen Baumann, *Paragraph 175: Über die Möglichkeit, die einfache, nicht jugendgefährdende und nicht öffentliche Homosexualität unter Erwachsenen straffrei zu lassen* (Berlin/Neuwied: Luchterhand, 1968).

9. *The Freud-Jung Letters: The Correspondence of Sigmund Freud and C. G. Jung,* ed. W. McGuire (Princeton, N.J.: Princeton University Press, 1974), 97, 125, 126. But about three years later in their correspondence, Jung let slip another slur. He was writing about a man named Römer, who was homosexual, and said: "He is, like all homosexuals, no delicacy." See ibid., 423.

10. See, for instance, S. Sadger, "Ist die Konträre Sexualempfindung heilbar?" *Zeitschrift für Sexualwissenschaft,* no. 2 (1908): 712–20. I thank Professor Steakley for bringing this essay to my attention.

11. The colleague was the Italian analyst Edoardo Weiss. See Edoardo Weiss, *Sigmund Freud as Consultant* (New York: Intercontinental Medical Book Corp., 1970), 9. On Tausk and his relation to Freud, see Paul Roazen, *Brother Animal* (New York: Knopf, 1969); K. R. Eissler, *Talent and Genius* (New York: Grove, 1971); and Neil Hertz, "Freud and the Sandman," in *Textual Strategies,* ed. J. Harari (Ithaca, N.Y.: Cornell University Press, 1979), 296–321.

12. Quoted by Nathan Hale, *Freud and the Americans: The Beginning of Psychoanalysis in the United States, 1876–1971* (New York: Oxford University Press, 1971), 339.

13. N. Hale, ed., *James Jackson Putnam and Psychoanalysis* (Cambridge: Harvard University Press, 1971), 87, 90, 91, 95, 117, 130, 137, 152, 153, 161, 168, 171, 189.

14. Ruitenbeek, ed., *Freud As We Knew Him,* 220.

15. Ernest Jones, *Free Associations: Memoirs of a Psychoanalyst* (London: Hogarth, 1959), 190.

16. *The Standard Edition of the Complete Psychological Works of Sigmund Freud,* trans. and ed. J. Strachey et al., 24 vols. (London: Hogarth, 1966–1974), 11: 9, 39, 33, 16, 17, 30, 31. I thank my student Andrew Tully, who made a comment in a classroom discussion that helped me to focus my ideas about the *Five Lectures.*

17. Martin Duberman, "The Therapy of C. M. Otis: 1911," *Christopher Street* (November 1977): 33–37.

18. Hale, *Freud and the Americans,* 346.

19. "A Letter from Freud," 786.

20. I follow John Lauritsen and David Thorstad, *The Early Homosexual Rights Movement, 1864–1935* (New York: Times Change, 1974); James Steakley, *The Homosexual Emancipation Movement in Germany* (New York: Arno, 1975); and Timothy Roe Lyman, "Homosexual Movements in Per-

spective: The Emergence of Homosexual Identity in Germany, 1900–1933"
(A.B. honors thesis, Harvard College, 1980). I thank Timothy Lyman for
his kindness in permitting me to read his excellent thesis.

21. *Standard Edition*, 7: 142.

22. *Standard Edition*, 11: 98, 99.

23. *Standard Edition*, 16: 304, 307, 308.

24. *Standard Edition*, 12: 145.

25. *Standard Edition*, 16: 308.

26. *Standard Edition*, 16: 307, 7: 145.

27. Quoted by Ronald Bayer, *Homosexuality and American Psychiatry: The Politics of Diagnosis* (New York: Basic Books, 1981), 28, 29. In my account of Rado, Bieber, and Socarides, I generally and gratefully follow Bayer. So perhaps I should note that I cannot follow his treatment of Freud. There Bayer goes wrong. He tends to accept that Freud believed what American analysts have said he believed.

28. Quoted in ibid., 30, 31, 34, 35, 36, 37.

29. This classification was also reflected in the attitudes of a substantial number of American health-care professionals. As late as 1971, just two years before the classification was rescinded, a study of a random sample of 163 such professionals in the San Francisco area (63 social workers, 50 psychiatrists, and 50 clinical psychologists) showed that only 64 percent overall were prepared to say that homosexuality wasn't an illness. See Joel Fort, Claude M. Steiner, and Florence Conrad, "Attitudes of Mental Health Professionals toward Homosexuality and Its Treatment," *Psychological Reports* 29 (1971): 349. One way of gauging the enduring force of American moralism may be to compare these results with those of a rather similar study done the same year in England. A random sample of 300 health-care professionals (150 general practitioners, 150 psychiatrists) showed that 94.3 percent overall were prepared to say that homosexuality was not an illness. See Phillip A. Morris, "Doctors' Attitudes to Homosexuality," *British Journal of Psychiatry* 72 (1973): 436.

30. Bayer, *Homosexuality and American Psychiatry*, 136.

31. Quoted in ibid., 138.

32. J. Marmor, ed., *Sexual Inversion* (New York: Basic Books, 1965), 2, 3, 4.

33. Robert Stoller, *Sex and Gender* (New York: Science House, 1968), 142, 143, 144.

Some Speculations on the History of Sexual Intercourse during the Long Eighteenth Century in England

1. E. A. Wrigley and R. S. Schofield, *The Population History of England, 1541–1871: A Reconstruction* (Cambridge: Harvard University Press, 1981). Of course, there has been *some* criticism. See, for instance, Peter Lindert, "English Living Standards, Population Growth, and Wrigley-Schofield," *Explorations in Economic History* 20 (April 1983): 131–55; and Louis Henry, "La population de l'Angleterre de 1541 à 1871," *Population* 38 (July–October 1983): 781–826.

2. E. A. Wrigley, "The Growth of Population in Eighteenth-Century England: A Conundrum Resolved," *Past and Present* 98 (February 1983): 121–50. Wrigley has reprinted this essay with little revision in *People, Cities, and Wealth: The Transformation of Traditional Society*, E. A. Wrigley (Oxford and New York: Blackwell, 1987), 215–41.

3. Wrigley, "Conundrum," 129.

4. Ibid., 131.

5. Ibid., 132; Wrigley and Schofield, *Population History*, 263.

6. Wrigley, "Conundrum," 131; Wrigley and Schofield, *Population History*, 255.

7. Wrigley, "Conundrum," 132, 133.

8. Ibid., 133; Wrigley and Schofield, *Population History*, 266, 254.

9. This may be the right place to remark that family limitation was practiced very seldom in preindustrial England and so registers virtually no impact macrostatistically. See C. Wilson, "Natural Fertility in Pre-Industrial England, 1600–1799," *Population Studies* 38 (1984): 225–40.

10. Wrigley, "Conundrum," 134.

11. Ibid., 142. Wrigley suggests that the currently available data on eighteenth-century English wage rates may be defective, and he may be right. But there is no reason to suppose that improved data would yield the conclusion that he wants.

12. See, for instance, E. P. Thompson, "Time, Work-Discipline, and Industrial Capitalism," *Past and Present* 38 (December 1967): 56–97.

13. Jean Louis Flandrin, *Families in Former Times: Kinship, Household, and Sexuality*, trans. R. Southern (Cambridge: Cambridge University Press, 1979); G. R. Quaife, *Wanton Wenches and Wayward Wives: Peasants and Illicit Sex in Early Seventeenth Century England* (New Brunswick, N.J.: Rutgers University Press, 1979); Alan Bray, *Homosexuality in Renaissance England* (London: Gay Men's Press, 1982).

From Thoreau to Queer Politics

1. Joel Myerson, ed., *Emerson and Thoreau: The Contemporary Reviews* (Cambridge: Cambridge University Press, 1992), 372, 373, 375, 389, 391, 400, 401, 395.

2. Ibid., 373, 388, 390.

3. Ibid., 399, 390, 384, 379.

4. Ibid., 423, 430. See also Michael Warner's comment on the "countless normalizing apologies for Thoreau," in his article "Walden's Erotic Economy," in *Comparative American Identities: Race, Sex, and Nationality in the Modern Text*, ed. Hortense Spillers (New York: Routledge, 1991), 159.

5. For some helpful thoughts on how the term "queer" is nowadays used and meant, see Lisa Duggan, "Making It Perfectly Queer," *Socialist Review* 22, no. 1 (January–March 1992): 11–31.

6. Henry David Thoreau, *The Variorum Walden and the Variorum Civil Disobedience*, ed. Walter Harding (New York: Twayne Publishers, 1968), 14.

7. Ibid., 127.

8. Ibid., 109.

9. Ibid., 108.

10. On the early history of this tradition of interpretation, see K. J. Dover, *Greek Homosexuality*, 2d ed. (Cambridge: Harvard University Press, 1989), 197–99.

11. Thoreau, *Variorum Walden*, 62.

12. Daniel Defoe, *Moll Flanders* (London: Penguin, 1989), 114.

13. Quoted by Stanley Cavell, *The Senses of Walden* (New York: Viking, 1972), 20. I believe myself to be much indebted to Cavell's luminous writings on *Walden*, particularly to his discussion of boredom.

14. Thoreau, *Variorum Walden*, 78.

15. Ibid., 82.

16. Paul Goodman, *Nature Heals: The Psychological Essays of Paul Goodman*, ed. Taylor Stoehr (New York: Free Life Editions, 1977), 219.

The Queering of Lesbian/Gay History

1. Stanley Fish, *Is There a Text in This Class? The Authority of Interpretive Communities* (Cambridge: Harvard University Press, 1980). See also Paul Gilroy, *"There Ain't No Black in the Union Jack": The Cultural Politics of Race and Nation* (Chicago: University of Chicago Press, 1991), 187.

2. Martin Duberman, Martha Vicinus, and George Chauncey Jr., eds.,

Hidden from History: Reclaiming the Gay and Lesbian Past (New York: New American Library, 1989), 1.

3. Jeffrey Weeks, *Coming Out: Homosexual Politics in Britain from the Nineteenth Century to the Present* (London: Quartet Books, 1977).

4. Carroll Smith-Rosenberg, "Discourses of Sexuality and Subjectivity: The New Woman, 1870–1936," in *Hidden from History*, ed. Duberman, Vicinus, and Chauncey Jr., 265.

5. John D'Emilio, *Sexual Politics, Sexual Communities: The Making of a Homosexual Minority in the United States, 1940–1970* (Chicago: University of Chicago Press, 1983), 248.

6. Lillian Faderman, *Odd Girls and Twilight Lovers: A History of Lesbian Life in Twentieth-Century America* (New York: Columbia University Press, 1992), 303–4.

7. Arthur Schlesinger Jr., *The Vital Center: The Politics of Freedom* (Boston: Houghton Mifflin, 1949).

8. For instance: "You're the top! / You're Mahatma Gandha. / You're the top! / You're Napoleon Brandy. / You're the purple light of a summer night in Spain, / You're the National Gall'ry, / You're Garbo's salary, / You're cellophane . . . / I'm a toy balloon that is fated soon to pop, / But if, Baby, I'm the bottom / You're the top!" See Robert Kimball, ed., with an introduction by Brendan Gill, *Cole* (New York: Holt, Rhinehart, and Winston, 1971), 124.

9. Weeks, *Coming Out*, 185, 189, 192.

10. My information about Boy comes partly from these queer students, partly from my own observation, and partly from Douglas Crimp, "The Boys in My Bedroom," in *The Lesbian and Gay Studies Reader*, ed. Henry Abelove, Michèle Aina Barale, and David Halperin (New York: Routledge, 1993), 346–49. For a commentary on the slogan "Just sex," see Michael Lucey, "The Consequences of Being Explicit: Watching Sex in Gide's 'Si le grain ne meurt,'" *Yale Journal of Criticism* 4, no. 1 (1990): 174–92.

11. I believe that the tone these queer students like best was also available, perhaps commonly so, in political polemic during the era immediately preceding Stonewall about thirty years ago. For instance, see Gore Vidal's comment in his afterword to *The City and the Pillar*, rev. ed. (New York: New American Library, 1965): "In any case, sex of any sort is neither right nor wrong. It is" (158). For another instance, here is the Philadelphia activist Clark Polak in the May 1965 issue of *Drum:* "Sex cannot be 'dirty'

because it cannot be 'pure.' It cannot ennoble one any more than it can debase. It is not, under some circumstances, 'good,' and under others, 'bad.'" Polak is cited by Marc Stein, "Sex Politics in the City of Sisterly and Brotherly Love," *Radical History Review* 59 (1994): 85. I should say that these students are less uncomfortable with immediately pre-Stonewall than with immediately post-Stonewall and liberationist politics.

12. Madeline Davis and Elizabeth Lapovsky Kennedy, "Oral History and the Study of Sexuality in the Lesbian Community: Buffalo, New York, 1940–1960," in *Hidden from History*, ed. Duberman, Vicinus, and Chauncey Jr., 431.

13. For my account of Queer Nation and of queer politics more generally, see "From Thoreau to Queer Politics," in this volume.

14. Donald Allen, ed., *The Collected Poems of Frank O'Hara* (New York: Alfred E. Knopf, 1971), 305. I am grateful to Steven Evans for teaching me much of what I know about how to read O'Hara. I have already indicated (see note 11) that my queer students feel less estranged from preliberationist than from postliberationist lesbian/gay politics. Their attraction to O'Hara, who died in 1966, is an additional illustration of what I mean. On another occasion I hope to write more about the relation or potential relation between the queer generation and the lesbian/gay generation of the 1950s and early 1960s.

American Studies, Queer Studies

1. For biographical information on Matthiessen, I rely on F. O. Matthiessen, *From the Heart of Europe* (New York: Oxford University Press, 1948); the Matthiessen memorial issue published just after his death, *Monthly Review* 2, no. 6 (October 1950); Louis Hyde, ed., *Rat and the Devil: Journal Letters of F. O. Matthiessen and Russell Cheney* (Hamden, Conn.: Archon, 1978); *Harvard University Gazette* (November 18, 1950); and the Matthiessen Papers, on deposit at Beinecke Library, Yale University.

2. Throughout Hyde's *Rat and the Devil*, the enormous importance of Skull and Bones in Matthiessen's life is obscured. Where Matthiessen refers to Skull and Bones in his manuscript letters, the editor usually removes the reference without comment.

3. F. O. Matthiessen to Russell Cheney, September 17, 1924 (Matthiessen Papers, Beinecke Library, Yale University).

4. See, for instance, F. O. Matthiessen, *Russell Cheney, 1881–1945:*

A Record of His Work (New York: Oxford University Press, 1947), 6. But there is an occasional hint that something is being withheld. For instance, Matthiessen says of Cheney, "he kept his inner life almost entirely unspoken" (5).

5. See especially John Lydenberg, ed., *A Symposium on Political Activism and the Academic Conscience: The Harvard Experience, 1936–1941* (Geneva, N.Y.: Hobart and William Smith Colleges, 1977).

6. Joseph and U. T. Summers, cited by Hyde, ed., *Rat and the Devil*, 12. For a report by another graduate student who perceived Matthiessen's homosexuality, see Lyle Glazier, "Homage to F. O. Matthiessen," *Fag Rag*, no. 24 (n.d.): 28–29. Glazier's essay is a little-known but beautiful and thoughtful tribute. It is also possible that some undergraduate students thought of Matthiessen as homosexual. The *Harvard Crimson*, the college newspaper run by undergraduate students, reported of Matthiessen: "his house in Kittery he shares with the artist Russell Cheney" (*Harvard Crimson* 104, no. 8 [September 28, 1933]: 1).

7. F. O. Matthiessen, *American Renaissance: Art and Expression in the Age of Emerson and Whitman* (New York: Oxford University Press, 1941), 610. On the bodily connotations of the term "renaissance," as Matthiessen uses it, see Jonathan Arac, *Critical Genealogies: Historical Situations for Postmodern Literary Studies* (New York: Columbia University Press, 1987), 162.

8. Matthiessen, *American Renaissance*, x.

9. On Matthiessen's inexplicitness, evasiveness, and indirection, see Jay Grossman, "The Canon in the Closet: Matthiessen's Whitman, Whitman's Matthiessen," *American Literature* 70, no. 4 (December 1998): 799–832. Grossman begins by pointing out that Matthiessen never once uses the word "calamus" in *American Renaissance*.

10. W. H. Auden to F. O. Matthiessen, June 27 (no year) (Matthiessen Papers, Beinecke Library, Yale University). See also Edward Mendelson, *Later Auden* (Farrar, Straus, and Giroux: New York, 1999), 165.

11. Charles Olson, *Call Me Ishmael*, with an afterword by Merton M. Sealts Jr. (Baltimore: The Johns Hopkins University Press, 1997), cited by Sealts, 145, 11, 14, 104. In a 1942 letter applying for a job in the Office of Strategic Services, Olson actually cites his research on Melville and the Pacific as a qualification. See Ralph Maud, ed., *Selected Letters of Charles Olson* (Berkeley and Los Angeles: University of California Press, 2000), 36–37.

12. Yvor Winters, *In Defense of Reason*, 3d ed. (Chicago: Swallow Press, 1943), 599, 590.

13. Leslie Fiedler, *Love and Death in the American Novel*, Anchor Books ed. (New York: Doubleday, 1991). Fiedler says so in his 1992 afterword (510), where he also acknowledges his indebtedness to D. H. Lawrence's *Studies in Classic American Literature*.

14. Fiedler, *Love and Death*, 12.

15. Stanley Cavell, *Conditions Handsome and Unhandsome: The Constitution of Emersonian Perfectionism* (Chicago: University of Chicago Press, 1990), especially xxxii, 6, 7, 104.

16. Lydenberg, ed., *A Symposium on Political Activism*, 6.

17. Robert Penn Warren to F. O. Matthiessen, September 8, 1947 (Matthiessen Papers, Beinecke Library, Yale University).

18. Irving Howe, review of F. O. Matthiessen, *From the Heart of Europe*, *Partisan Review* 15, no. 10 (October 1948): 1125–29.

19. Draft letter, F. O. Matthiessen, March 3, 1949 (Matthiessen Papers, Beinecke Library, Yale University). There is no evidence that Matthiessen completed and sent this letter.

20. Quoted by Hyde, ed., *Rat and the Devil*, 367. Matthiessen also left personal notes for each of his Skull and Bones friends on his desk at his Boston apartment.

21. *Webster's New Collegiate Dictionary* (Boston: G. C. Merriam, 1961), 55.

New York City Gay Liberation and the Queer Commuters

1. On the homophile clubs, see John D'Emilio, *Sexual Politics, Sexual Communities: The Making of a Homosexual Minority in the United States, 1940–1970* (Chicago: University of Chicago Press, 1983); and Marc Stein, *City of Sisterly and Brotherly Loves: Lesbian and Gay Philadelphia, 1945–1972* (Chicago: University of Chicago Press, 2000). For an overview of the sixties, see the still useful Sonya Sayres, Anders Stephanson, Stanley Aronowitz, and Frederic Jameson, eds., *The 60s without Apology* (Minneapolis: University of Minnesota Press, 1988). On the riot at the Stonewall Bar, see Martin Duberman, *Stonewall* (New York: Dutton, 1993). Among the community studies are George Chauncey, *Gay New York: Gender, Urban Culture, and the Making of the Gay Male World, 1890–1940* (New York: Basic Books, 1994); Elizabeth Lapovsky Kennedy and Madeline D. Davis, *Boots of Leather,*

Slippers of Gold: The History of a Lesbian Community (New York: Routledge, 1993); Esther Newton, *Cherry Grove, Fire Island: Sixty Years in America's First Gay and Lesbian Town* (Boston: Beacon Press, 1993); and Stein, *City of Sisterly and Brotherly Loves.* For two perspectives on New York City's Gay Liberation Front, see Terrence Kissack, "Freaking Fag Revolutionaries: New York City's Gay Liberation Front, 1969–1971," *Radical History Review,* no. 62 (spring 1995): 104–34; and Karla Jay, *Tales of the Lavender Menace: A Memoir of Liberation* (New York: Basic Books, 1999).

2. D'Emilio, *Sexual Politics, Sexual Communities,* 176–82.

3. For Bishop's view of Ginsberg, see George Monteiro, ed., *Conversations with Elizabeth Bishop* (Jackson: University Press of Mississippi, 1996), 35; and Brett C. Millier, *Elizabeth Bishop: Life and the Memory of It* (Berkeley and Los Angeles: University of California Press, 1993), 323. For Rorem's view of Burroughs, see Ted Morgan, *Literary Outlaw: The Life and Times of William S. Burroughs* (New York: Henry Holt, 1988), 7. I deduce O'Hara's view of Baldwin from scattered indications and from the Baldwin joke O'Hara played on Terry Southern. See Terry Southern, "Frank's Humor," in "Homage to Frank O'Hara," ed. Bill Berkson and Joe LeSueur, *Big Sky* 11/12 (1978): 112–16.

4. "Allen Ginsberg: An Interview by Gary Pacernick," *American Poetry Review* 26, no. 4 (July–August 1997): 26.

5. For an account of the long-term development of colonialist tropes and values, see Anne McClintock, *Imperial Leather: Race, Gender, and Sexuality in the Colonial Contest* (New York: Routledge, 1995). Greg Mullins, "Writing Interzone: American Expatriate Literature in Postwar Tangier" (Ph.D. diss., University of California, Berkeley, 1997), explains how the Tangier group, including Paul Bowles and William Burroughs, relied on their status as Americans to secure sexual opportunities and more while they lived in Tangier. Mullins also provides an analysis of their fiction. I am much indebted to his dissertation, which has been published in revised form (*Colonial Affairs: Bowles, Burroughs, and Chester Write Tangier* [Madison: University of Wisconsin Press, 2002]).

6. On the persecution of queer Americans during the Cold War, see, for instance, John D'Emilio, "The Homosexual Menace: The Politics of Sexuality in Cold War America," in his *Making Trouble: Essays on Gay History, Politics, and the University* (New York: Routledge, 1992), 57–73; Kennedy and Davis, *Boots of Leather, Slippers of Gold*; Nan D. Hunter,

"Identity, Speech, and Equality," in Lisa Duggan and Nan D. Hunter, *Sex Wars: Sexual Dissent and Political Culture* (New York: Routledge, 1995), especially 124–28; and William N. Eskridge Jr., "Privacy Jurisprudence and the Apartheid of the Closet, 1946–1961," *Florida State University Law Review* 24, no. 4 (summer 1997): 703–838.

7. See, for instance, Robert K. Martin, "Scandal at Smith," *Radical Teacher*, no. 45 (1994): 4–8; Barry Werth, *The Scarlet Professor: Newton Arvin, a Literary Life Shattered by Scandal* (New York: Nan A. Talese, 2001).

8. Louise S. Robbins, "The Library of Congress and Federal Loyalty Programs, 1947–1956: 'No Communists or Cocksuckers,'" *Library Quarterly* 24, no. 4 (October 1994): 365–81.

9. Millier, *Elizabeth Bishop*, 210.

10. For details on Bowles's engagement with the Library of Congress, see the correspondence between him and various Library managers on deposit in the Paul Bowles/Moroccan Music Collection, American Folklife Center, Library of Congress.

11. Fred L. Standley and Louis H. Pratt, eds. *Conversations with James Baldwin* (Jackson: University Press of Mississippi, 1989), 202, 256, 233.

12. James Merrill, *A Different Person: A Memoir* (New York: Alfred A. Knopf, 1993), 5, 96, 97, 3.

13. Millicent Dillon, *You Are Not I: A Portrait of Paul Bowles* (Berkeley and Los Angeles: University of California Press, 1998), 216.

14. Allen Ginsberg, *Selected Poems, 1947–1995* (New York: HarperCollins, 1996), 64.

15. Standley and Pratt, *Conversations with James Baldwin*, 15, 178.

16. Paul Goodman, *Five Years* (New York: Brussel and Brussel, 1966), vii, viii.

17. He says so in the preface to a 1982 reissue of *The Spider's House*. See Paul Bowles, *The Spider's House* (Santa Rosa, Calif.: Black Sparrow Press, 1982), 1.

18. James Baldwin, *Giovanni's Room* (New York: Dial Press, 1956), 3, 221, 223. For indications of a generation's absorption in Baldwin, see Richard Goldstein's introductory comment in Richard Goldstein, "'Go the Way Your Blood Beats': An Interview with James Baldwin," in *James Baldwin: The Legacy*, ed. Quincy Troupe (New York: Simon and Schuster, 1989), 173; and Leonard Andrews Jr., "Personal Reflections on Gay Liberation from the Third World," in "Stonewall Fifth Anniversary Issue," *Fag Rag/Gay Sunshine*

(a combined issue of *Fag Rag* no. 9 and *Gay Sunshine* no. 22) (summer 1974): 38–39. Some Liberationist readers were, however, annoyed that the protagonist of *Giovanni's Room* was white rather than black and that Baldwin, in his own contemporary comments on the novel, had seemed to deny that it was centrally concerned with homosexuality. Roger Austen, for instance, spoke with distress of what he took to be Baldwin's "obligatory dash of obfuscation." See Roger Austen, "U.S. Gay Fiction: Historical Overview," *Gay Sunshine*, no. 32 (spring 1977): 13.

19. One reader, John Ashbery, thought that these earlier poems were overly confessional. Commenting on the volume in which they appeared, which was titled *A Cold Spring*, Ashbery said, "the poet's life threatened to intrude on the poetry in a way that didn't suit it." Ashbery's comments are reprinted in *Elizabeth Bishop and Her Art*, ed. Lloyd Schwartz and Sybil P. Estess (Ann Arbor: University of Michigan Press, 1983), 203.

20. Elizabeth Bishop, *Questions of Travel* (New York: Farrar, Straus, and Giroux, 1965), 3, 4, 5, 6, 7, 8, 12, 23, 34, 35–44.

21. Millier, *Elizabeth Bishop*, 355, 409.

22. For example, *Gay Sunshine*, *Fag Rag*, and *Gay Community News* all focused in their various ways on outreach to convicts and prisoners.

23. See, for instance, the first New York City GLF statement, as published in its newspaper, *Come Out*, in September 1969 (*Come Out! Selections from the Radical Gay Liberation Newspaper* [New York: Times Change Press, 1970], 5).

24. This poem was first published in Donald Allen's immensely influential anthology, *The New American Poetry, 1945–1960* (New York: Grove Press, 1960), 253–54. It was reprinted in Frank O'Hara, *Odes* (New York: Tiber Press, 1960), n.p.; and then reprinted again in *The Collected Poems of Frank O'Hara*, ed. Donald Allen (Alfred A. Knopf, 1971), 305. For evidence of O'Hara's impact, see Berkson and LeSueur, "Homage to Frank O'Hara," Stuart Byron, "Frank O'Hara: Poetic Queer Talk," and Rudy Kikel, "The Gay Frank O'Hara," in *Frank O'Hara: To Be True to a City*, ed. Jim Elledge (Ann Arbor: University of Michigan Press, 1990), 64–69, 334–349; and Russell Ferguson, *In Memory of My Feelings: Frank O'Hara and American Art* (Berkeley and Los Angeles: Museum of Contemporary Art, Los Angeles, in association with the University of California Press, 1999).

25. Winston Leyland, ed., *Gay Sunshine Interviews*, vol. 1 (San Francisco: Gay Sunshine Press, 1978), 13, 14, 118, 119.

26. Winston Leyland, ed., *Gay Sunshine Interviews*, vol. 2 (San Francisco: Gay Sunshine Press, 1982), 196–97; Taylor Stoehr, ed., *Nature Heals: The Psychological Essays of Paul Goodman* (Highland, N.Y.: Gestalt Journal Publication, 1977), 219.

27. *Dear Paul, Dear Ned: The Correspondence of Paul Bowles and Ned Rorem*, introduction by Gavin Lambert (Elysium Press, 1977), 117–18.

28. Gary Fountain and Peter Brazeau, eds., *Elizabeth Bishop: An Oral Biography* (Amherst: University of Massachusetts Press, 1994), 330.

29. Standley and Pratt, *Conversations with James Baldwin*, 84, 197.

30. *Come Out!* 59. In addition to speaking and writing, the Liberationists sometimes also tried to lend a hand in what they saw as decolonizing work outside, as well as inside, the United States. For an account of the Liberationists' initial support for the Cuban revolution, of the willingness of some Liberationists to participate in it personally, and of their eventual exclusion from participation, see Ian Lekus's unpublished paper "¿Quién Es Más Macho? Homophobia, Machismo, and Ideology on the Venceremos Brigades." Lekus's Ph.D. dissertation, now underway at Duke University, will also be pertinent. It is titled "Queer and Present Dangers: Homosexuality and American Antiwar Activism, 1964–1973."

31. Ferguson, *In Memory of My Feelings*, 133.

Permissions

"Freud, Male Homosexuality, and the Americans" was originally published in *Dissent* 33, no. 1 (winter 1985–86): 59–69; reprinted with permission by *Dissent*.

"Some Speculations on the History of Sexual Intercourse during the Long Eighteenth Century in England" was originally published in *Genders* 6 (1989): 125–30. Copyright 1989 by the University of Texas Press; reprinted with permission by the University of Texas Press. All rights reserved.

"From Thoreau to Queer Politics" was originally published in *Yale Journal of Criticism* 6, no. 2 (1993): 17–27; reprinted with permission by *Yale Journal of Criticism*.

"The Queering of Lesbian/Gay History" was originally published in *Radical History Review* 62 (1995): 44–57; reprinted with permission by *Radical History Review*. Copyright 1995 MARHO, The Radical Historians' Organization.

Excerpt from *Girls on the Run* by John Ashbery, copyright 1999 by John Ashbery; reprinted by permission of Farrar, Straus and Giroux, LLC, and Carcanet Press Limited.

Excerpts from "Questions of Travel," "Arrival at Santos," "Brazil, January 1, 1502," "The Burglar of Babylon," "Song for the Rainy Season," "Squatter's Children," and "Twelfth Morning, or What You Will" from *The Complete Poems, 1927–1979* by Elizabeth Bishop; copyright 1979, 1983 by Alice Helen Methfessel; reprinted by permission of Farrar, Straus and Giroux, LLC.

Excerpts from "City Midnight Junk Strains" and "America" from *Selected Poems, 1947–1995* by Allen Ginsberg (New York: HarperCollins Publishers, 1996). "City Midnight Junk Strains" was first published in *Planet News* (1963); copyright 1963, 1996 Allen Ginsberg. "America" was first published in *Howl, Before and After,*

Henry Abelove is coeditor of *The Lesbian and Gay Studies Reader* and author of *The Evangelist of Desire: John Wesley and the Methodists*. He has taught in history and in English departments, and is now Willbur Fisk Osborne Professor of English and director of the Center for the Humanities at Wesleyan University.